look inside

His Story – Her Story – Their Story

Moon Shadow Lodge

Robert Hugh and Francie Brown

Look Inside Inc.
Knoxville, TN

2nd Edition – Interactive Color
ISBN: 9781686411045

Look Inside Inc.
A US Registered 501(C)(3) Non-Profit
www.ClickToLookInside.com

Editor: Terra M Goosie
Illustrated by Jerry Helm

Printed in the United States of America

Table of Contents

Interactive Edition

Follow and listen along to the real people read their own story.

The entire book is in print here, so this is not required, but with adding a simple *free* Smartphone App, the experience of *Moon Shadow Lodge* comes to life with hearing the real people share their own story as you listen or read along.

To do that, in this 2nd edition, we have added what's called, *QR Codes* for any smartphone to play an audio or video recording.

4 Simple Steps:

1) On your smartphone, go to your App Store or Google Play Store.
2) Search QR Reader
3) You will have several 'free' options. The free ones that show small ads are often much faster.
   a. A couple of popular Apps as of this publishing:

       i. Apple: *QR Reader for iPhone, QR Code Reader and Barcode Scanner*
       ii. Google Play: *Free QR Scanner, QR Code Scanner*

4) Install the App and test by Scanning the Welcome Video QR Code on the right, which is also on the front cover!

Introduction

Acknowledgements

We would like to thank:

Our Mentors and Coaches
Dan and Becky Allender
Phil and Gina Cohen
Buddy Cooper
Mike and Beth Hamilton
Jim and Wendy Johnson
Zach Clark, Rachael Clinton, Jason Manarchuck
Bill Prenatt and Jay Stringer

Editor Terra Goosie
Illustrator Jerry Helm

Team Brown
Josiah, Jacob, Jordan Elizabeth, Justin, Sarah and Baby Ariadne

To the entire cast of the Moon Shadow characters who made this possible and have cheered us on. Sharing your stories, strength, courage, heartache and beauty have blessed us. We will never be the same.

We are forever grateful to each of our donors who have fed and clothed our family and moved this mission forward. You have enabled us the honor of doing story work and reaching thousands of men and women. We are also grateful for the Suggs family and their Moon Shadow Lodge where we had our first and over thirty retreats.

Dedication

John and Phyllis Stone

This book simply would not have happened without the support of John and Phyllis Stone. Their own obedience, humor in the midst of the storms and love, sustained and moved us forward. Many afternoons and evenings were spent in the home of John and Phyllis. We would show up on their doorstep with tears or heartache and they would kindly listen. Then their stories would begin, followed by the laughter and encouragement that would lead us to press on.

Thank you, John and Phyllis, for sharing your stories and your hearts with us. You are continuing to impact the eternal here on earth even though you have already left us.
We love you.

Foreword

Coming out of our bedroom, into the kitchen, I found my teenage son fanning smoke from his burning fried potatoes. The smoke alarms finally sounded. Out of nowhere, I called out, "Clang, clang, goes the fireman! Clang, clang, goes the fireman!" and stopped in my tracks, frozen and puzzled at such an odd thing for me to do. "Where on earth did that come from." I said out loud and went to fan the other detector with a pillow.

As I fanned the smoke and pondered, it finally came over me. *Frankie the Brave Fireman*. At forty-seven years old, I'm calling out a quote from a 1956 children's book I hadn't seen or read in over four decades. With joy of the memories of Frankie, my hero, I then began to sing the song that came with the flimsy, *Read-a-Long* record. The smoke cleared, alarms shut off and then I darted to the family computer and opened YouTube. There it was. I pressed play, with my kids and Francie standing behind me. I couldn't wait to see what happened next. When the unique sound of that scratchy record began, in an instant, my mind and even body quickly felt like a toddler again.

 As you might imagine, *Frankie the Brave Fireman* is about a young boy who dreams of being a brave fireman in his hometown. He is told he is too young and small to be a fireman and is discouraged. Then, one day, it all changes with a raging, tall building fire downtown. With the regular fireman at a different fire, Frankie springs into action to save a trapped dog from the top floor while the whole town watches his bravery. He becomes the hero of the town.

As a toddler, I listened to this record while turning the pages well over a hundred times. Why? Because everyone loves a good story. They make up the very fabric of who we are.

Whole tribes and nations have been founded by narratives, and even centuries later we are still a storytelling culture. The US alone spends over

12 billion dollars per year at the movies and authors publish over 1 million books. We can't get enough of stories.

The fact is, we are biochemically designed to hear stories and to tell stories. Expert, Louis Cozolino, says there are scientific reasons as to why stories are so important to us. He describes,

> *"Although stories may appear imprecise and unscientific, they serve as powerful tools for high-level neural network integration. The combination of a linear storyline and visual imagery woven together with verbal and nonverbal expressions, activates circuitry of both left and right hemi-frontal lobes. ...It is likely that our brains have been able to become as complex as they are precisely because of the power of narratives".*

Understanding that story is important is crucial but secondly, we need to *know* our own before we can start to inspirationally share them. Many feel they don't have a story because they've "lived a normal life." Dr. Dan Allender, says this ideology is flawed. He says, *"We live in a cruel, broken world. At some point, you've had to encounter outrage or hurt. No one has the human capacity to live a normal life".*

We've had the honor of walking along side over a thousand men and women the past ten years and each with their own unique stories. There are specific types of events that shape much of the direction of our lives. This book was designed with each of those in mind.

This narrative is based on real people and their real stories. These are foundational stories that were explored in a coed group, retreat setting. With their permission and encouragement of this project, we are honored to share them with you. Welcome to the Moon Shadow Lodge.

Rob and Francie Brown

Peter Pan Records *Frankie the Brave Fireman. 1956.*
Cozolino, L. *The Neuroscience of Psychotherapy.* W.W. Norton and Co. 2017.
Allender, D., *To Be Told Conference* Chicago, IL, 2012.

Moon Shadow Lodge

Mary

Since Mary could remember, there was always an underlying hope in her marriage to Greg that she would somehow 'get it together.' Ten years ago, when they lived in Alabama, she'd been to her first women's conference, called 'Real Woman,' at the Buck Creek Lodge. That Friday night, the women arrived to a grand mahogany lined entrance, Colorado pine tables, exposed beams, and marble floors in the dining hall. Greg had thought maybe she should stay home because of the weather, but Mary was determined to make it. When she arrived, Mary called home, and Greg told her that there had been a tornado nearby and he and the kids had gotten in the bathtub. For a moment, Mary felt guilt for leaving but then was even more convinced that her being there was the right thing. It was two nights, forty women, great speakers, laughing, stories late into the night, and a sense of arriving to a new life.

She had gone to the conference with such excitement, confident that it was the great beginning in learning how to be a better wife, mother, and friend. But on the lonely drive home, what stuck in Mary's mind more than anything else was the realization that most of the women there were already friends. It had been hard leaving Greg and the two little ones behind, and after that weekend, she never told Greg that within a few days, she actually felt more alone and confused than before she'd gone.

This spring, Mary made another attempt to move forward in her life and accepted an invitation to join a women's study at a local church. She quickly read the book the women were reading and was excited but anxious about going. There were a few women she already knew attending the study, but Mary thought they had it all together and wondered why those women were even going. The study was twelve weeks, and the first night during introductions, there were many general references to struggles, but some were pretty raw. The second meeting Mary was assigned an older woman, Ruth, as a mentor to disciple her during the week. Since Mary had two small children, they met at her house on Friday mornings. They would 'check-in' with each other with light conversation and a devotion here and there, and by the sixth week, Mary had drifted away from being honest about her struggling marriage and life. She wondered if others were covering up too or if it was just her. She decided it must be her.

For Mary, getting married was so exciting at first. Now, ten years, three moves, in-law conflicts, two more kids, and four women's conferences later, she finds herself in a world that's more complicated, stressful, empty, and clouded with confusion. And at the age of thirty-nine, she wonders if there's anything more. If this is all there is.

Today, Mary is driving from her home in Nashville to a Story Retreat in the Smoky Mountains. Greg planned ahead to work on his computer with headphones on so Mary has plenty of time to herself to think. "When will we ever get there?...Maybe this isn't for me?...Maybe we should turn around?...I think my stomach isn't feeling so good. Maybe I'm sick, and I sure don't want to get others sick." And finally, the inevitable truth, "Please God, I've been alone for so long; deliver me from this solitary confinement." It was that place of being deeply alone, with only a thin slice of hope, that kept her minivan moving down the highway.

As the GPS brought them further, it was time to turn south. She went down a few country roads, and a tunnel of cedar trees opened wide into a pasture that was as far as she could see. It ended at the foot of mountains to the east. The caps were slightly covered with a fog that captivated her, and for a moment her heart skipped as it began to beat faster. Greg was in another world in his computer and making one last phone call.

As Mary reached the final, four-way stop on Old School House Road, the road signs were missing, and the GPS had ended a mile back. Which way to turn, she wasn't sure. Mary could see a sign in the distance that straight was a dead end, to the right looked like a road to being far more lost than she already felt, and the left was a road lined with oak and pine trees that got more and more narrow off into the distance. Mary turned left and drove. As the road narrowed to one lane, her heart was at full pace. "This must be the way," she thought. Just before giving up and turning around, she saw off in the distance, on the crest of a hill, in the middle of a green meadow, a lone standing cabin. Smoke was billowing out of the rock chimney into the evening sky, and as she gazed, she stopped the car and took a deep breath. Mary whispered to herself, "Here we are. So this is where it begins..."

Moon Shadow Lodge

Greg ended his call quickly before being disconnected in the mountains.

As Mary got out of the car, she saw a friendly face on the porch. It was Francie. She and Rob led the co-ed weekends together, and Mary recognized her from the video. Francie had talked to her several times over the phone, and if it weren't for Francie's encouragement, Mary would have backed out. In that last call, Francie said, "Mary, whatever men and women are supposed to be there, will be there. I don't know where you are with this, but there is one thing I do know; this retreat, for certain, will not be the same without you." Mary didn't know how to respond to that. She couldn't recall a time where another woman considered her important. A stranger at that! Rob met Greg at the van to help carry their bags. Standing at the top of the wooden steps, Francie placed Mary's lanyard on her neck, looked her in the eyes with a smile, and said, "Mary, I'm glad you're here. Welcome!"

The place is called the Moon Shadow Lodge. Surrounded by mountains on three sides, it sits in the middle of fifty acres of green grass surrounded by pine trees. The inside is dressed out with hand-hewn pine and cedar that had been cut from clearing the surrounding land over thirty years ago. About a hundred yards from the cabin is an old barn where the sawmill still sits that had been used to cut the wood when the cabin was raised.

As with most mountain lodges, at the center is a magnificent stone fireplace. It is one of the largest Mary has ever seen, and it had been hand-built with stones carried from a stream close to the barn. It not only provided warmth from the forty-degree weather, but somehow, too, a mysterious comfort and security that most everyone desperately needed. Especially Mary.

Mary settled in over the first hour, got her materials, picked out her bunk in the women's quarters, and some of the people introduced themselves. Greg went out back to help get the campfire set for the night. Someone asked Mary if she could help stir the spaghetti and unbox the Texas Toast. That was a lifesaver for her. Standing around alone was frightening, but as more arrived, she was amazed to hear people talking about their lives so quickly. Seeing the looks on their faces and warm embraces left Mary speechless as she quickly turned and looked away.

It was soon six o'clock and time for dinner. Spaghetti sounded great after a long day. Mary went through the line and found the seat at a round table with her name on it next to Rob's. She introduced herself to John, Karen, and Ryan. Greg's seat was at the other table with Francie, a country looking man named Brock, and two ladies named Angela and Lisa. As they had dinner and small talk, Mary wondered who these people really were and how they got there.

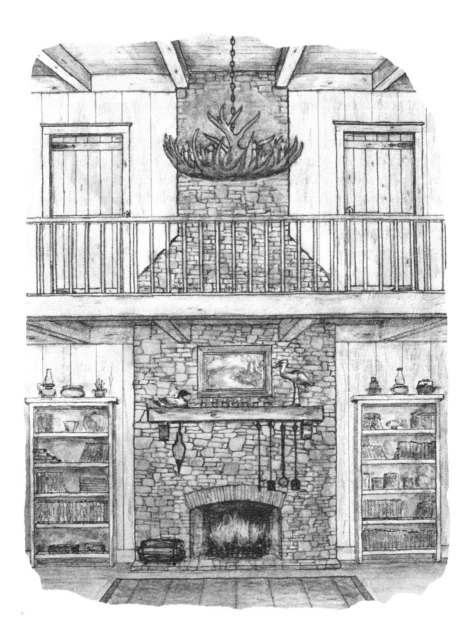

John

Auto Reply: "In a meeting. Can I call you back?" At the pace John is running, that will likely be the inscription on his headstone. He is the Executive Vice President of Operations and part owner of Allied Steel Works, a progressive and high-tech steel company. After most of the metal companies in the US have failed, three partners have figured out how to do the impossible. John's other partners are the visionary and sales guys. John, however, is the one who makes it all work, and the company is quickly approaching $100M in revenue. Hanging on John's office wall is a newly framed magazine cover: Forbes – "Fast 50" – Allied Steel Works.

At networking events, the country club, even at the grocery store, women would talk about what a handsome, great man, husband, and father John Glass is. There is only one significant problem. John is not sure he wants to live anymore.

John hasn't gotten to the point of developing a plan, but he has been daydreaming of how his family would be able to move on quite well without him, especially with their accumulated wealth and life insurance.

He had fallen in love with his high-school sweetheart and married Susan right after graduating from CalTech. They have four kids: two in college and two still at home. Susan is a strong support for John, but is often busy with the kids, the club or at their west-side church. Most of the country club members go to Olivet Community Fellowship.

John rarely stops because when it gets too quiet, he starts having those bad thoughts, so the best solution has always been to stay moving until he collapses from exhaustion at the end of the day.

John also likes to play as wide open as he works. Three times per year, the whole family goes snow skiing in Aspen. They also love to water ski, so an hour from home, they have a cabin on the lake with a competition ski boat. John's success has carried him and Susan on business trips to Spain, Germany, Mexico, Brazil, China, and even Moscow.

John has operated for twenty years as if he could conquer the world, but a dark cloud of fear has set in over the past three years. A fear of, "If people only knew," that he can't seem to shake. This summer, his best friend, Dan from college was passing through town, and they met at Earl's, a local, quiet coffee shop.

Being at CalTech, John had been overjoyed to go to college but also had had severe anxiety. He would toss and turn and sometimes shake in his bed at night. A few nights the first two weeks, he yelled out and woke Dan up. In the dorm, most of the guys, chocked full of hormones, got dressed wherever and often ran around in just their underwear. But John would always dress in a private stall in the bathroom. Dan never asked questions, but in a matter of a few weeks, John felt safe enough to be open and honest with Dan. On a Saturday morning, they sat on the edge of their beds facing each other. John shared, "I know it's strange about my clothes. Two days before I thought I was going to start fifth grade with the rest of my friends, I was sent away by my parents to a private school where the leaders believed discipline was a top tenant. My severely crooked teeth are enough to deal with, but the scars on my body, I never want anyone to see." Before John could think about it, he pulled up his shirt and showed Dan one of the scars on his side. That was the day they became best friends.

And it was there at Earl's Coffee shop that Dan shared with John about going to the retreat.

Karen

Being the leader of the children's ministry at New Life Church was no easy task. In total, there were over one hundred kids. Karen and her husband Todd were there at the Stone's home when it had started. It was a Bible study and a dream. Karen would volunteer to watch the kids, and as the dream of planting a church sprouted, it began to grow. People kept coming, and so did their kids. That had been fifteen years ago, and after all those years, Karen is still the children's ministry leader, and Todd is leading the middle school youth program. With their own kids grown, they both feel unnoticed, and bitterness is setting in because no one has offered to relieve them from their volunteer positions.

At sixteen, Karen had gotten pregnant. She was then living with Aunt Betty who was a comfort because she had her first son as a teen as well.

Karen only got behind one semester of high-school and finished just after turning nineteen. Being a single mom and waitress, Karen found it was hard to make ends meet with bills, baby food and diapers, doctor appointments, and a broken-down car.

Tips were enough to survive, but there was always a thin line where if anything went wrong with the car or if her baby got sick, she had to ask other people for money and those favors had run out. It was a hot summer Thursday night in 1986 when everything changed.

Along with Karen, Penny was a waitress at Willy's Steakhouse. She had been there longer than Karen but had a brand-new car and sure seemed happy. Karen went on break and sat with Penny in the back.

It was just the two of them when Karen said, "Wow, girl! Those are some slick wheels you're driving. How can you afford that working here?"

While lighting up a cigarette, Penny explained, "This is my day job. My real job is Friday and Saturday nights. I make as much money in six hours as I do in forty here."

Karen asked, "So, what do you do?"

"I'm a dancer," she casually remarked.

"Where?" Karen inquired.

"Frank's Gold Club," replied Penny.

"You're a stripper? Are you kidding me? You can't be serious!" she half shouted in surprise.

"Listen, it's such easy money. Over $200 a night for dancing to six songs in three hours. And, if Jack likes you, he lets you work holidays. There was one Valentine's Day where I made $500. It was a Tuesday night!"

Karen already knew how to party and dance, but not like this. She was a mom. But, if something like this worked out, she could get a better car and new clothes for her baby girl. After some coaching from Penny and a few stiff drinks, Karen was able to do it. A month later, she was driving a nice car with a baby seat in the back. She had figured out a way to make her life work.

After a year of dancing, Karen became so depressed about it that one night she was out behind the club dumpster crying and feeling like throwing up. In the parking lot, a Monte Carlo was parked close by. The driver was a newer customer, drank a lot, and looked as lost as she did.

Karen looked to the sky and cried out, "I don't want to do this anymore!"

The man got out of his car, shut the door, and walked close to check on her. When she saw him, he looked right in her glistening eyes and said, "Then don't."

At that moment, she felt oxygen fill her lungs like she had been slowly drowning. She just needed permission to quit, even from a stranger. She asked, "What's your name?"

"Todd."

Ryan

While Rob and Francie were setting up inside the lodge, a loud car came down the gravel road. Ryan arrived early in his beat-up Mitsubishi with a guitar in the front seat and his gear in the back. His stress was obvious. He carried everything in one load: his sleeping bag, pillow, guitar, and army rucksack. At the age of twenty-eight during times of trouble and loneliness, Ryan has become comfortable hiding behind his guitar. He has it with him everywhere he goes.

Seven years ago, Ryan was newly married and attended his first men's sexual purity meeting at church. Ryan slipped in the back of the room to a chair in the corner. Young, slim, blonde wavy hair, an earring, and sparkling blue eyes, he curled up in his seat, his head mostly down. The leader, Frank, stepped through the circle of eighteen men to shake hands with the newest attendee and asked everyone to make room in the circle. The meeting began, and everyone did their check-in. Most every check-in was an update on the week's battle with lust although some would share about their anger or alcohol problems. Most men were convinced they were sex addicts from the book they had read, but no one really knew for sure. Everyone was just excited about finding a place to fit in with something real. When it got around to Ryan, he shared that Matt, the pastor, had pushed him to attend.

Ryan was working minimum wage as a breakfast-shift dishwasher at Shoney's. Rene worked full-time as an office assistant at an insurance agency on the north side of town. Deeply struggling, Ryan and Rene's marriage counseling was not going well. He was frustrated because the two pastors were focusing on communication problems. "She's kind of a bitch. That's the problem," he said to the other men. "She nags me every day. Says I am lazy, and I play too many video games. It's not like I don't have a job. When it gets bad, I just go to Jeff's house and game with him or out to Irish Times with my buddies."

After the meeting, the men went to Smoke-N-Barrel on Main Street. After a beer and a dart game, Frank asked Ryan what video games he liked.

Ryan said, "Call-of-Duty is what Jeff and I play the most. I'm in the top 5% of all registered players."

"Wow!" Frank was surprised. "So, how much do you play?"

He responded, "I get home about 11am and game until Rene gets home from work at 5:30. On weekends, I go to Jeff's house and a couple other guys come over, too. There's all-day tournaments on weekends that we compete in."

Frank said, "What do the pastors think about the gaming?"
"They don't really think it's a big deal. They say we just need to get better at listening to each other, pray, and read the bible together. Then things will get better."

Ryan came to the meetings for a few months and then began having schedule conflicts.

A year later, the meeting had moved across town, and on a snowy December night, Ryan walked in shining bright and greeting the guys he already knew. During check-in, he shared he had finally gotten a divorce due to 'irreconcilable differences,' changed churches, and had a new job waiting tables at Calhoun's.

Within two years, Ryan had had his fill with Knoxville. He got a call one Friday morning from an old friend. Bryan Simmons was his camp counselor during his teen years and found Ryan on Facebook. It was an easy sell talking Ryan into a job at the new Elkmont Brewery. Now, as the assistant manager, Ryan is being groomed to be the top man in charge. He's also been dating Christine, a nurse's assistant at the local hospital, for three years. She is attending night school pursuing her nursing degree, and between their schedules, they often get nights and days mixed up but see each other as often as they can.

Ryan's best friend from Dallas talked him into coming this weekend.

Getting Started

Dinner came to a close, and just before seven, there was a five-minute warning that the evening activities were to begin. Everyone gathered their materials and quickly grabbed their seats.

There were welcoming announcements, an explanation of ground-rules and format, guidelines and a general flow of the weekend, and then it was time for introductions. All ten men and women were sitting in a circle, and it was time to share in no more than a couple of minutes why each person was here and how everyone was feeling. They started to the right which made Mary last.

Angela started, "Where am I right now? I'm still stressing about my ex-husband taking care of my girls, the stuff I didn't get done at work today, and my son's graduation next weekend. I suppose I feel anxious and really not here right now, but I will be soon."

"I'm Brock, and I saw these retreats online a year ago, and the next day there was one last open spot at a men's retreat in Orlando, so I grabbed a flight and left the farm. It changed my life. Now, I am here for the co-ed experience and a lot more anxious than being at a men's retreat. But, I'm pretty excited about this weekend."

Everyone else was either excited or nervous, but mostly both. Finally, it was Mary's turn, "Honestly, I am crazy nervous and afraid. My husband, Greg, came to one of these, and it has clearly impacted his life, but I just don't know if there's much hope for me." Mary finally spoke what many of them were honestly thinking.

In what seemed like high-definition, slow motion, Rob offered a challenge, "I'd like you to commit to being as honest with yourself and with us as you possibly can. No BS. You can lie through this whole weekend. But, maybe, if you're like me, you've gotten tired of hiding and lying your way through life. But you're not fooling anyone. And you're only going to get what you put in to this weekend."

That sent a chill in the air. "What in the world does honest mean?" Karen thought with a bit of panic.

It was time to get started. At about the same time, everyone in the room sat up straight, like good students do, opened their books, and clicked their pens.

The smell of rich spaghetti sauce and garlic bread was gone, but in the silence of the great room, everyone could smell and hear every drop of the strong coffee brewing and the crackle of the fire.

Francie said, "This exercise, no one else will ever see your answers. I want you to write as best you can...what are you hoping for this weekend?"

Karen breathed deeply and tried to relax. Her being at this retreat right now, at this point in her life, was Class A evidence that there must be a better plan for her life. Reflecting on when she was a little girl, she had many hopes and dreams. But now, at the age of fifty-two, she had come to believe her dreams were just foolish.

Like looking into a Polaroid photo in his mind, Greg remembered clearly now, at five years old, the many nights gazing through his three-pane, floor to ceiling, bedroom windows into the night sky. The feeling of knowing that someday he would be rescued. But, he could also hear the yelling, screaming, hitting, and banging coming from his parent's room that was next to his. His parents fought a lot and often well into the night. When the sounds of those arguments and the sounds of his own crying would still penetrate the pillow that covered his face and ears, he would crawl out of bed, kneel in front of his lower window, stare at the stars, and dream of a day where he would be far away. Far away to a place where there were no tears, no fighting, no hurting. With a loud pop from the fire, he opened his eyes and could almost feel the moonbeams from long ago that would shine on his face as the tears dried.

Getting Started

The next words from Francie were, "If each of us provided a definition of faith, we would have ten different ones. Here is a working definition for this weekend. Faith is built on stories where there was a rescue and shattered when there was not."

This rang true for Mary as she reflected on her growing up and her friends over the years. She's had faith in those who have been there for her and not for the people who haven't. But still, in her haunting of deep loneliness, she feels a strong hope of connection in the company of these women and men. This was different than anything she had experienced before.

Five people took turns reading the values for the weekend. They were clarity, honor, kindness, safety, and growth. Rob commented, "It's almost impossible to know what these really mean by looking at words on paper, so guess what? You are going to experience these this weekend."

They did a few other activities and then had open sharing time for anyone who felt comfortable to do so. Brock was amazed how much he related with each person, even the women. Lisa had silent tears. John gazed out the window while Brock was biting his fingernail. People were beginning to become themselves. Angela was taken by how what each person shared seemed so sacred. After a bathroom break, there was one last activity for the evening.

Everyone returned, and Mary leaned back in her seat on the sofa and with a few deep breaths finally began to forget about her fears and like a windshield wiper clearing away a light rain, she let go of the cloud of stress she had brought along with her.

Francie said the night would end with story time, and that this would not be like a story time they'd experienced before. She would be the facilitator for the group as Rob shared a story of his own. Francie explained, "What we are doing is exploring a story now. This is what each of you will be doing tomorrow, and half of you will be in my group and half in Rob's. Now, everyone needs to understand that this is a very real story of Rob's. This is not a teaching example. It's only the third time in his life he has ever shared this in front of anyone. We believe that every story must be treated as sacred. And when on sacred ground, we take our shoes off. So let's all slip them off." They did. It was somewhat strange, but the entire mood of the room changed in seconds as a thick cloud seemed to lift before they even began.

The General

Sitting in a semi-circle and after a few deep breaths, Rob began to read. It was what he called his, "Basketball Story - The General." John listened on the edge of his seat as the story began in the office of the legendary basketball coach for Indiana University, Bobby Knight. A few didn't know who that was, but it seemed like it must be a big deal. Rob was fifteen and a sophomore on Columbus High School's JV basketball team. His coach decided to take him along to IU on a Saturday morning. Rob had dreamed since he was a boy about playing basketball at IU and that one day he might play for Coach Knight in the great Assembly Hall. Rob sat on one of the couches and listened for an hour to his basketball coach and Coach Knight talk about many things: kids, grandkids, his coach's wife's cancer, Coach Knight's pending divorce, and basketball. Rob wasn't sure why they were there at first or why he was, but it became clear the two were close friends, and this must be what friends do. Rob stopped reading his story for a moment, then looked back down.

The story flashed forward three months from the majestic Assembly Hall at IU to the exciting night his high school varsity team won the state regional championship. Holding his hand-written story, the paper began to shake a bit after he read, "Then it was time to hit the showers." Ryan's heart began to beat faster. Lisa slowly pulled back into the corner of her couch cushions, and John looked down and stared at the floor. The story came to an end with Rob scrubbing and scrubbing with soap after five of the varsity players thought it would be fun to urinate all over him in the shower while the others laughed and laughed.

There was bone chilling silence. Rob was tapping his foot and gazing out the window. John kept his head down and thought, "Oh my, what are we supposed to do now? What does someone say?" Angela's eyes were bugging out, and Ryan stiffened up and crossed his arms. It was so quiet that everyone could hear Lisa slowly pull the last Kleenex out of the box. Mary partially hid herself behind Brock. Finally, every eye in the room locked onto Francie.

With Francie leading, the next fifteen minutes were spent exploring every angle of this story. The rest offered comments and a few questions. For sure, no one wanted to mention the shower, but Francie wasn't going to let it go and didn't. "Rob, when you realized what the other boys were doing, what did you do?"

Rob seemed quick to respond, "I put my head back in the shower and started washing my hair again. And I just washed with my eyes closed until everyone was gone."

"So you never saw anyone?" she asked.

"Well, the first time I heard someone giggle, I wiped the soap from my eyes and turned to look. And there they all were, naked, peeing on me and laughing. I couldn't believe it... the looks on their faces."

"What?"

"They were having so much fun while they pissed all over me. I thought they were my friends."

"It was a long time washing yourself until everyone left. When it was finally over, what was going through your mind?"

"That I just wanted to get out of there." Rob sat there frozen but breathing and finally finished. "And, that no matter what I do, I'll never fit in."

The last Kleenex was full of Lisa's tears. Ryan still sat silent. John's racing, problem-solving mind stopped as Mary and Greg glanced at each other, both knowing very well the deep desire to belong.

Francie paused for a moment, "Rob, as I look around, you seem to be fitting in with us." Everyone nodded. "In fact, you fit perfectly with us, and we are so honored you would allow us to be with you tonight. This has been really special." She finished with a summary and a challenge for Rob to consider. Then time was up.

At the end of the exploring time, everyone clapped for Rob, and then both he and Francie opened the floor for comments or questions regarding what they just experienced in Story Group.

There were a few clarifying questions, and then Karen spoke, "Growing up, I never played sports, so at first I thought it would be hard to relate. Wow, was I wrong. It was like it was my story, and I've not played basketball a day in my life."

John followed, "So this is what you mean by story exploration? I must admit, I was super excited and then really freaked out. Frankly, after we explored it, the significance of the story wasn't at all what I thought it was about. The cruelty was obvious, but the shame and loss of hopes and dreams was not obvious to me."

Then Francie asked, "Ryan, why did you never say anything? Where are you?"

He replied loudly, "Frankly, I was so pissed I just wanted to beat the hell out of those guys! I didn't think it would be helpful to be pissed off in front of everyone."

With a tear welling up, Rob replied, "Wow, Ryan. I had no idea. I can't even begin to say how good that makes me feel. In this moment, I've gone from believing from your silence, you thought my story was stupid, to having something I never had. A friend to fight for me, to look out for me, to have my back." Rob looked right in Ryan's eyes, "Ryan, thank you."

It was then, everyone seemed to be able to breathe again. Especially Ryan.

Campfire

It was to be lights out at 11, and everyone was free to hang out at the campfire, play games, or go to bed. Mary was exhausted and said good night. Francie, Brock, and Angela set up the card version of Monopoly at the game table. Everyone else went out to the fire.

Ryan was put in charge as the coffee man for the weekend, and Greg was the designated fire man. He had stacked up logs in a square, log-cabin style formation in the fire pit. He was quite proud of his creation. However, his pride quickly faded when he began the struggle of lighting it. Before long and with Karen's help, the fire was roaring. Karen loved camping as she had gone many times as a youth leader at her church.

Everyone went and got a chair off the deck and set them by the fire. Rob had gone far off to the road to call and check in on his kids. It was quiet for a good while as the fire cracked and roared up into the black of the night sky.

"Wow, look at these stars," Ryan said with wonder in his voice. "It's been years since I've been able to see stars like this."

It was so dark in the field around the fire pit that you could see the flickering shadows of the flames against the side of the lodge.

John noted, "I really don't know what it is, but there's something about a fire that's not like anything else. It's captivating. It seems to leave behind space and time."

Ryan picked up a stick on the ground, got out a knife from his pocket, and began to whittle. Greg leaned forward in his chair to warm his hands near the fire.

After a few more random comments from all of them, Lisa finally spoke, "Rob's story really hit home for me, and I'm not sure why. Frankly, I thought I was coming here for one reason. But after that story, it's clear I'm here for something else, and I don't even know what it is."

Ryan replied, "Me too."

"I was amazed by Francie," Karen said. "I wouldn't know what to do or say if someone shared a story like that with me. Honestly, when I first got here, there was something that rubbed me the wrong way about Rob. He seemed too nice. Here he is a leader and helping haul luggage. I could barely stand it. Before story time, I didn't like him, and now I see him a lot different. I am so damn judgmental of people...especially women. Sorry Lisa," she chuckled.

"Oh, I get it," Lisa responded. "I grew up with three brothers. I actually prefer being around men. It's not easy for me to be around women."

'Pop' cracked the fire as Karen stomped out a burning ember in the grass.

Greg spoke, "Well, I grew up as a city boy with five sisters, and I'm the youngest."

"Whoa, that's rough," John interjected.

Greg went on, "Playing with dolls and being the only boy student in my sisters' make-believe classroom was my role. I didn't play sports, so I didn't get much interaction with boys except when I went to my cousin's house out in the country. I loved going there. A pond for fishing, motorcycles, bareback horse riding, and hunting. They had huge German Shepherds though that were chained in the garage most of the time and would bark right in my face. Being out here in the wilderness reminds me of those times."

Ryan added, "I've never rode a horse before."

John recounted, "My sister had a show horse. Sis was the special one. Still is."

Getting Started

Over the next hour, the sharing passed like the cool night breeze, and the fire burned down to glowing hot embers. John called it a night and headed to bed. Within fifteen minutes, the rest got up and carried their chairs back to the deck.

Lights out.

The Story

When Ryan woke up in his bed, he could smell coffee and biscuits and somehow felt a sense of being home, which was something he'd not known since he could remember. It had been a very long time since he had slept that well.

By 8am, everyone was up, dressed, and ready for breakfast. After fixing plates, everyone sat around the cabin in different seats. Two of the women sat on the floor in front of the fire. John walked outside to the still smoldering fire-pit from the night before. Brock followed him out to smoke a cigarette. By 8:30 it was time to get the day going as Francie rang the old fashioned school bell that was hanging next to the front door.

After they all got settled in, Rob began, "In a little while we are going to turn you loose to write your own story, but last night I got to share one with you, and this morning Francie is going to share one of hers with me facilitating. Like mine, this is one that Francie has only shared a few times and the first time in a co-ed group. It is very real. She has learned a lot from this story, but this is one where there is still more to learn. Are we ready? Francie?"

The Barn Story

"Yep. Let's do it." She picked up a paper from under her chair and sat it in her lap. As she began to read, the story started off with a bright, beautiful, Friday morning. School hadn't started back yet, and she was at home on their family farm babysitting while her parents were at work. Fixing breakfast and lunch while watching a soap opera was a summer favorite. She looked out the window at her brother and his friend running by laughing, but she didn't think much of it. A few minutes later, her seven-year-old brother ran inside screaming, "The barn is on fire. The barn is on fire. We were trying to play a trick on you with a smoke bomb."

Getting Started

Francie looked out the back door and saw raging flames barreling out of the top of the barn. This Indiana barn was three stories tall and could hold over three hundred pigs in the bottom floor. Francie scrambled to phone for help and tried to find the number that was hanging on the wall, but her eyes couldn't focus, and her hand was trembling so badly that she decided to call her dad at work. There was no answer. She then reached her mom. "I'm on my way."

Running outside, she remembered their favorite dog was in the barn and ran to try and get him, but the neighbors had arrived and held her back as the barn was completely engulfed in flames. People could see the smoke from the raging fire miles away. Everyone was standing at a distance watching the barn burning and could feel the heat on their bodies.

While Francie read her story, everyone could also feel the heat from the fireplace as though they were there standing in front of the barn with her. John thought about the beauty of the fire last night and now the shock of destruction of fire in Francie's life. Her story came to an end with a finale explosion of fireworks from the hayloft before it collapsed. It was as though everyone in the room could hear the fireworks and see the barn collapsing. As Francie spoke the last word, she slowly looked up. A heavy silence fell across the room. They were all in shock.

Rob began a moment later by thanking Francie for sharing this story with the group and then asked her to tell more about the farm. Then the group began to engage. There were several good questions, even a couple Francie had never thought of before. Some things were uncovered. There were also two handicapped adults working in the greenhouse that morning. Boys used the hayloft to hide Playboy magazines. The barn was never rebuilt, and her parents divorced a year later.

Then Angela asked, "I didn't catch how old you were."

Francie thought a moment and seemed to be doing some math in her head. With a bit of shock on her face, she said, "So, I had to be ten."

Angela gasped out loud. Then said with her eyes wide open, "I'm sorry. I shouldn't have done that. I just thought you were a lot older than that. Oh, my. Oh, my." Francie herself had believed she had been thirteen or fourteen.

A few moments later, John softly asked, "How could you blame a ten- year-old?"

Francie sighed, "I suppose you can't."

Lisa questioned, "Do you ever remember your parents blaming you?"

Francie thought for a moment. "No, I don't. I guess I've just blamed myself all these years."

There was a moment of silence, then they clapped and thanked Francie for sharing. She took a deep breath and smiled as they stood up for a break. Several went to get more coffee, and several went straight to the bathroom. Brock went to smoke. Lisa and Karen grabbed their jackets and walked out into the open field. Ten minutes later the bell rang for them to gather again as Brock put out his half-smoked, cigarette.

My Story

It was time for everyone to head out and spend private time writing their own stories. Before they were dismissed, Rob and Francie both shared snapshots of examples of other stories they had written and explored in other groups. As each went through their examples, words like break-up, sex, classroom, funeral, addiction, playground, divorce, and pornography stirred up a whirlwind of thoughts and emotions in everyone's minds. In those moments, it became clear to everyone that no story was off limits. They were all dismissed to go find a private place to write.

John had determined since he was far from home, and with encouragement from his best friend Dan, he was going all in with a particular story from his private school.

Karen had felt for many years her mother's death was the most significant story in her life. She had been to many counseling sessions over it, and it had seemed to make no difference. She had never cried or gotten emotional about it since it happened forty-two years ago. She thought, "Oh well, maybe if I follow this approach, it will lead somewhere different." She ended up naming her story, 'Strawberry Plains.'

Ryan wrestled with this. He packed up a chair and hiked across the field and up the side of the mountain behind the lodge. About half-way up, he found a flat spot behind the stump of a tree. He set up his chair, sat down, and kicked back with his feet up on the stump. After taking in the sunshine, he reached carefully into his jacket pocket. Before breakfast, he had grabbed a small box of matches and asked Brock for a single cigarette in case there was a time he needed one. This was that time. He hadn't smoked since he worked at Shoney's. He fired it up with one strike of a match, closed his eyes, and waited for inspiration of some kind. Time went by. He saw what looked like a bald eagle flying above the open field and not long after a doe and fawn on the edge of the woods grazing. He thought maybe those were signs of some kind, but nothing came. He closed his eyes again after putting the leftover cigarette butt back in his pocket. A light breeze blew a strong familiar smell his direction and he looked to the right. A strong wind or storm must have recently blown down two pine trees because the splits were fresh. The smell of pine surrounded him, and it was then that the story came. 'The Pinewood Derby.' He grabbed his pen as the story began to pour out, and fast it came.

When it came to the story that was on Mary's mind, it was not what she was thinking on the drive there, but this morning it was obvious after Francie said, "...or maybe it's simply a story that you just haven't been able to get out of your mind, and you're not sure why." It became crystal clear. Mary set up her chair by the fence line facing a cow pasture and began to write, 'Thanksgiving at Aunt Carol's.'

For some, the time alone was an eternity, but for others it passed in a blink of an eye. Brock had finished fifteen minutes early and was walking around and back smoking again at the ashy fire pit. Angela couldn't help but wonder if he had even written a story as she scrambled to finish hers. Slowly but surely, one-by-one, they all began to file back in to the lodge for lunch.

Lunch was an Italian chicken dish, rolls, and a hearty salad. Everyone was hungry. The sun was bright out and made it warm enough for most everyone to sit outside for the thirty-minute break.

As lunch came to an end, Rob announced, "You all need to be in your seats in five minutes before we split into groups."

Francie began, "Well, welcome back, all of you. I hope you had some special private time and a good lunch. Now we have reached the time you've been waiting for or freaked out about. Whichever fits. I will tell you that hundreds of people have done this, and you're going to be ok. This is going to be one of the best things you've experienced."

That was a relief for many to hear.

Angela thought, "Maybe I'll be the first not to be ok."

Everyone was to focus on exploring the written story and not ask leading questions. Rob said, "We will not be giving out any ribbons this weekend for asking the best or most profound question. Most often, the best questions are the simplest ones."

Francie explained, "Every one of you has been asking the same questions over and over in your mind for years. Exploring is about bringing out new questions and discovering clues you haven't seen before. Although it has happened before, there will likely not be a magical miracle for you this weekend. So remember the goal is progress."

The Sunroom

A comfortable, private spot with windows on three sides had been set up for Rob's group, and Francie decided that her group would meet outside.

Rob, Mary, John, Ryan, and Karen all found seats in a circle and looked around the room. Ryan crossed his legs and began tapping his foot, Karen sipped some more coffee, and John leaned back waiting to see what happened next. Mary sat up straight with her story in hand as if she was waiting to start.

Rob, "Well, Mary. It looks like you are ready to go."

"Yep, let's get going. I'm ready."

The others seemed relieved that Mary was going first.

Rob said, "Well, typically I don't let the person who 'wants' to go first, go first. Are you sure, Mary?"

"Yes," she answered.

Rob announced, "All right, then let's do it."

So Mary began to read.

Mary - "Thanksgiving at Aunt Carol's"

In Queens, NY, Thanksgiving is when the cold begins to arrive. As I stepped out of our '72 El Camino onto the gravel driveway, I looked around and saw quite a few of my family members were already here. At 12 years old, here we are, another Thanksgiving at Aunt

Carol's. It would be the same old crew – my dad's sisters, their kids, and some grandkids. All laughing and telling loud stories and off-color jokes, waving their beer cans around in the air telling stories with wild gestures just like every other holiday. I walked up the sidewalk in my orange and yellow dress that my mom had sewn, then up the stairs and onto the front porch. I grabbed the broken handle of the storm door, and the heavy, wooden front door with its forever cracked glass windows was already open.

Of course Aunt Carol had kerosene heat. The crowded house would be hot. At least there would be fans running. It was always fun to talk into them with my brother and cousins. We would practice our robot voices today. As we all walked into the living room, the loudness got louder. All the aunts and uncles and cousins noticed our arrival and greeted us loudly, all trying to talk over each other. I struggled through the awkward hugs and told them all I was "fine" when asked. I looked around for my cousins, Bonnie and Kenny. They were close enough to my age, so we shared the kids' table.

I wandered the house a bit and found Bonnie in her room down the hall. The dirty pale green walls were brightly lit with both sets of curtains wide open. The sunshine streamed in onto her bed and all the junk scattered on the floor. She greeted me and started talking about herself. Again. Bonnie never wanted to know about me. She was just always looking for an audience. Oh well, it was better than sitting and sweating on the hot couch in the hot living room, watching some boring old time movie playing too loud on the TV. I sat on her desk chair and listened to her high school escapades. At 15, she knew more than I did. At least she seemed to think so. I was smarter than her, and I knew it, but I kept my mouth shut. We weren't arguing test scores.

After a few minutes, she closed her bedroom door and said, "Hey, I wanna tell you about my boyfriend." Her whispering told me that Aunt Carol didn't know something about him or didn't know about him at all.

I said, "Sure," and watched her intently.

She began to tell me all about making out with this 20-year-old man! My thoughts ran wild. How could she date a grown man? Why would she want to? Whatever they were up to surely was not good.

My racing thoughts began to take off when she stood there and said, "And he hugged me from behind and reached around me and grabbed my boobs like this." She stopped to demonstrate as if I wouldn't understand. My mind raced again. Why would she tell me this? Didn't she know you were supposed to be married before doing that stuff? Was she going to wind up pregnant? I'd never had a boyfriend, but I knew enough from the teaching of my mom and my church to see where that kind of behavior was headed. I must have looked shocked or like I thought it was gross, because she stopped there. We got called to eat. I left the room, my head spinning, trying to wrap my mind around all that she had told me.

I walked to the kitchen and loaded up my plate in a daze. I set my plate down on the card table in the living room that us kids used and went in search of a drink. I pushed open the broken storm door on the side of the house and went out onto the patio. The smell of charred meat hit me. My two cousins, Bobby and Vinny, manned the grill, waving around a long handled spatula and beer cans as they talked and laughed loudly, ignoring the chops burning on the grill. They didn't notice me, just kept on drinking and laughing as they burned up our family tradition. The coolers were up against the house. First one, all beer. Second one, all beer. The third held some soda cans, so I chose a Sprite and went back inside.

I ate my meal with my brother, Paul, and with Bonnie and Kenny. We laughed and joked together and messed around with our food, as always. I almost got my mind off what Bonnie had told me but not quite. The party went on. People coming and going, and eating off the table set with food that had been left out all day. Gross. Most everyone sat around and drank and smoked and talked too loud. Some of their stories were funny. Some I didn't understand, but I just didn't really like how as the night went on, the volume went up and the alcohol went down.

At last it was dark. My oldest cousin, Vinny, had fireworks out in the garage leftover from the Fourth of July. My brother loved helping blow stuff up. My mom didn't like it, but my dad always said, "What's the harm? Let him have a little fun." I hated it. Every bit of it. What if someone got hurt? We were nowhere near a hospital. And my dad had been burned on his arm before by a roman candle. The worrywart in me kicked into full gear while most everyone was drunk. So we all went outside to the huge backyard. The kids were given sparklers. I took one just so I didn't have to argue with a drunken cousin why I didn't want to get burned. I waved it around gently until it went out then stood off to the side unnoticed. As the drinking went up, so did the danger of the fireworks. It seemed like an eternity of people trying to light something, laughing too loud because they couldn't get it lit, and then running crazy once the fuse was lit – beer in one hand, lighter in the other. The booms went through my body and the whole neighborhood. I stood afraid at a distance and watched until the last of the noisy fire hazards was gone. We filed slowly inside, said our goodbyes, and collected what was left of the scalloped potatoes. After saying goodbye too many times, we headed back out to the car. Mom drove home because Dad needed to "rest his eyes." At least I had survived another Thanksgiving at Aunt Carol's.

Karen sat with memories flickering of the many drunken holidays of her childhood and her best friend's boyfriend who was always flirting and looking her up and down. Ryan couldn't help but remember the time he accidently blew up the neighbor's flower pot with M-80 firecrackers. John's wheels were quickly turning in a panic to try and figure out the solution to all this.

Rob asked, "This is a great story to bring to the group. Why this story?"

Mary gave the group an explanation as to why she picked this story and further one-liners on her family holiday traditions. The other group members asked questions about cousins, fireworks, and her mom and dad.

Finally, Rob asked, "Is it ok if we spend some time in Bonnie's room?"

"Sure," replied Mary.

With one question, Mary began speaking a mile a minute about Bonnie. It became clear that on one hand Mary looked up to Bonnie and even dreamed of being like her, and on the other hand she couldn't stand Bonnie and spoke about how much smarter she was than her.

Finally, Rob had a chance to ask, "Can you share more about what you did know about sex, Mary?"

Pause.

"Yeah. Frankly, Bonnie was the only person I ever learned anything about sex from. My parents never told me or taught me anything about sex. In fact, when I was in middle school and started my period, it was my best friend, Amy, that helped me figure it all out. For sure, our 'fire and brimstone' church made it clear that having sex, unless you're married, would send you straight to hell. Just the word 'sex' sent fear through me when I was young."

Karen inquired, "How did you feel when Bonnie told you about her date?"

"Of course I was confused and shocked, but at the same time I was also fascinated and then felt dirty...and still do."

Rob asked, "I know this is really hard, but I want you to think a moment and answer this question. Is it true that sex is bad?"

After a pause and shifting in her seat, Mary responded, "No. It's not."

Rob pressed in. "My last question: If you were to give yourself a grade for sex from when you were in school, what would it be?"

With passion in her voice looking out the window, "An F."

"How about now, Mary? What would be your grade now?"

Her head slumped to a stare in the center of the floor. In almost a whisper, she said, "The same."

"And, you are a good student, aren't you Mary?"

She looked up at Rob, "Yes. Yes, I am."

"Yes, you are a good student, Mary. And as of right now, in the group with us, you are getting an A," Rob said with a warm smile. He continued, "You have made great progress, and this is exciting. There is much hope for you. You are so brave to share this, especially in a co-ed group. I know I can speak for John and Ryan when I say we are honored that you've invited us to walk with you in this. We will make more progress tomorrow."

Everyone looked at Mary with smiles and a sense of a job well done. She sat back in her chair, took a breath, and deeply exhaled. She had feelings of being exposed and yet the hope of people caring for her. She hadn't felt this safe since she was thirteen with her best friend, Amy.

John - "Oak Park Academy"

Everyone took a few deep breaths, and then it was time for the next person. John said with a smile and his right leg bouncing, "All right, I'll go." Then he flipped his book inside out to where he had written his story. "Here we go."

 When I was seven, we moved to Oak Park, Illinois, just outside of Chicago because my dad got a new job. By the time I was eight, my parents had discovered a start-up private school. Most of the teachers were women, and the main leader was a man named Brian Baskin. It was a school that was "set apart from the world," they said. The school started out in Brian's basement but soon evolved into a small school meeting near the Frank Lloyd Wright home and studio. My earliest memories of the school were good. It started with a strong sense of community and some joy.

Slowly but surely, contact with the outside world began to disappear. Television, newspapers, magazines, and almost all radio were not allowed. Eventually all other schools became bad as well. There were thirteen students in my class, seven boys and six girls including my brother. We went to school and had no contact with kids outside our school.

The "principles" of the school were also to be followed at home. This was very important. When I was eight-years-old, we were not allowed to get presents for Christmas because we had "bad attitudes or had not behaved well." We had a chocolate pie in lieu of presents, and the money that would have been spent on gifts was donated to the school. Brian would teach about perfection and his responsibility to present us as perfect students. Bad behavior became defined as much more than normal childhood issues. A wrong word or perceived attitude became worthy of discipline. Failure to accurately memorize or show your work that was assigned became a serious offense. Over time things became increasingly unpredictable.

It all went from bad to worse when Ms. Clinch arrived. She and Brian were always unified. Ms. Clinch quickly became the face of discipline for the school. It seemed she had been wild in her prior life and was taking out her guilt and frustration on us. She was occasionally nice but often angry. It seemed like she targeted my brother and me more than the other students.

On one particular day we were beginning our day as usual. Someone was to volunteer to recite the school pledge, so I stood up and began to speak out loud. I do not know what I said or did that created the reaction, but Ms. Clinch came and grabbed me and pulled me out of the classroom, across the lawn to the kitchen. I knew what the kitchen meant as I had been there before, but she seemed to have an especially high level of anger and energy this day.

The usual tool of punishment was a long stick on bare skin. She had me pull my pants down and pulled me across her knees. She proceeded to hit me with the stick until it broke. I screamed and cried. She yelled, but I'm not sure what. This day left me with bruises and scrapes across my rear end and back. Evidence of this event was still present on my lower back until I was in high school.

The normal process was that punishments at school were followed by more punishment at home. I never really understood if this was done to reinforce the punishment or if I was being punished at home because I had created an issue at school. Sometimes the punishment at home was not another spanking. Being deprived of normal food and given bread and water was common. Often these home-based punishments were prescribed by the school. This time, my Mom let me have milk instead of water, but it felt like she was risking the wrath of the school to be kind to me.

Although his face was blushed, John sat in his seat like a proud school student. Mary's heart rate went up and blood began to boil. Ryan was frozen with his mouth a bit open. Rob reflected on his several trips to Principal Adams office to get his ruler rapping on the back of the knuckles and seemed to check out for a moment. Karen knew the switch whipping all too well from her step-mom, but her mind swirled at the thought of this man wearing a $100 golf shirt having a story like this. "How could I be so wrong about this guy?" she wondered.

"John, you are so brave to share this story with us. What an honor this is. Where are you right now?" Rob asked.

He responded, "Well, after all these years, my best friend from college encouraged me to hit this head on. The past few years, my time at the academy has been coming up in my mind like a dark cloud that won't leave, and I don't know why. I've spent forty years trying to forget it."

Ryan was curious, "So was there anything else that went on like that?"

John replied, "Yeah, there was, but this was the worst day, especially since I didn't even know why it was happening. I still have the one mark on my side. The rest of them healed up over time. I had really crooked teeth, but after I got my first job, I saved up money for braces. That was a lifesaver."

It seemed like a random comment, but he did smile, and his teeth clearly sparkled.

He went on, "From that experience, I am always on edge. I always have been. But, it definitely made me focus harder on my studies and staying out of trouble. It probably helped me be the first college graduate in my family. But even now, having to speak in front of people is like a near death experience. I tell my business partners that when it comes to speaking, I'd rather be in the coffin than giving the eulogy." Everyone laughed and slowly got quiet.

There were questions about the principal, Ms. Clinch, and John's classmates.

Then Karen asked, "So how could your parents let this go on?"

John recounted, "Like I said in my story, it started out pretty good. Everyone got sucked in, and then it got out of hand. My parents originally came from Denmark and didn't even graduate from high school. They just wanted the best education for me." As he said this with a bit of pride, Mary's eyes bugged out.
Ryan, leaning his chair back on two legs, said, "John, I'm really sorry that all happened to you. That's a real crappy hand you were dealt."

John nodded slowly, "I suppose it could have been worse."

At that point Mary couldn't hold it any more, and her steam kettle blew. "I just can't get over this! How on earth could a mother let this happen to a child? This is wrong! This is so wrong I can barely stand it! I want to go into that school and get that boy out of there."

Karen snapped, "I'd go in there and kick those people's asses! Especially, that woman!"

John sat up shocked and seemed to sober up as he watched the women respond. "That's what has always bothered me. Not knowing why my parents punished me or didn't take us out of there. My dad was always

39

busy, and mom just wanted everyone to be happy with her. I guess they just chose the people at school over me. Now, I must admit I was a kid who had a really hard time sitting still. They expected everyone to be responsible and focused. I wasn't one of those kids."

Rob chimed in, "John, now let me get this straight. Every nine-year-old boy struggles to sit still. That is quite normal. Can you imagine yanking a boy out of the classroom and beating him for not sitting still?"

"No! Never," John retorted.

Rob responded, "That's exactly right. It is so wrong. That should never happen to a nine-year-old."

As Rob said that, John noticed Karen, Mary, and Ryan shaking their heads in agreement.

Mary had settled down since her last outburst, "Yeah, every mom, dad, and teacher should protect their children. I'm so sorry they didn't, John."

At that, John sat silent and tears began to fall.

"Thank you, John," Rob said, and they all took a deep breath.

Karen - "Strawberry Plains"

Karen had waited so she could check John out. Since she arrived, she had her eye on him. His fancy clothes and tan leather loafers with no socks made her want to puke, and she really hoped he would NOT be in her group. And of course, he was. Just by looking at him, she was convinced he was a "fake, uppity asshole." She was mostly quiet during John's turn from total shock and guilt of her critical judgement. Even with her head spinning from the evaporation of her preconceived notions, she didn't feel any more hopeful about herself, but she did feel better that these other people had issues.

"Well, let's get it over with. Here goes. I called it, 'Strawberry Plains.'"

I was eleven at the death of my mom's husband, Elmer, my stepfather. My mother decided she now had time and room in her life for my sister Tammy and I to live with her and no longer just visit on weekends.

So, we switched schools and moved from the apartment to a small trailer in Strawberry Plains off Flint Gap Rd. Tammy and I each had our own rooms, and my small bedroom was off the kitchen and separated by a bathroom. We lived on someone else's farmland and had access to multiple acres of land to run and explore, and we treated cows like giant pets.

Because my mom worked a lot of hours as a waitress and when not working was out partying to medicate her pain from losing a man she really loved very much, I was in charge. My great-grandmother, Mattie, was living with us because she had heart trouble and surgery. Although she didn't seem to be fragile at all, she must have been because she was dramatic with confrontation with my mom and my Aunt Dottie when she was staying with us and would often ring her hands and act as if her heart would fail her at any moment. She smelled like snuff.

My mother was in the process of grooming me for a domestic life. She gave my sister and me $7 each per week and an extensive list of responsibilities that were inspected daily by my mom or my aunt. If they were not done to their satisfaction, $1 was promptly removed for that day. I actually enjoyed this and pursued doing all my chores to perfection so as to not lose that dollar.

Meanwhile, because I left my school on the west side of town, a school full of wealthy and best dressed kids and entered a school out in the country where my claim to fame was being the new kid, I was instantly popular. The academic bar was not super high, so I was also the smart kid. I was given the job of class monitor over a class of eight-year-olds. I always played cool games with them from 7:45 until 8:15 until the teacher arrived. I was his pet and was loved by all the kids. I joined the band class of four students. Every day, I loved to play my flute, and no one ever had to tell me that I needed to practice. Sometimes, my family members would say, "Give it a rest Karen!" and I would for a little while.

February 14th, 1976, I was up at 6AM and had all my Valentine cards ready to go. I was showered, dressed, and ready way ahead of schedule. Mom had not come home in the night, but that wasn't that unusual. The phone rang and I answered. It was Pete. I knew Pete because he had been in law enforcement with my stepfather. His voice sounded grave and flat and he said, "Karen, honey, I don't want you to go to school today. Your mom's been in a car accident, and she's in the hospital."

I was irritated, and before I knew it, blurted out, "She's dead isn't she? Just tell me the truth."

Pete answered, "Just don't go to school."

I went and woke up Tammy while my grandmother was sitting in the living room rocking back and forth in the big black leather chair wringing her hands and whining, "Linda's dead, I just know it. Linda's dead."

There was a knock at the back door, and there were two women and a man. The women had on long skirts with their hair up in buns, and the man was in a suit. They said they were from some church. I knew my mom never went to church, so I was irritated at their presence, but I made a pot of coffee and began to make a batch of silver-dollar pancakes for everyone. Everyone looked pretty lost and not sure what to do with themselves.

Then my dad arrived. He looked a little haggard and didn't say a word. He got really huge trash bags and started cramming all my stuff in them. I got really angry and started screaming at him while I fought to take my things out of the bags. "My mom needs me! I need to stay here for when she gets home!" I gave up the losing battle, and my hot, wet tears of anger and sadness got cold as I ran out the front door and looked out over the cow pasture trying to calm the pain that was consuming my head and chest.

While standing at the fence, to my surprise, I saw my other grandmother, my dad's mom, waiting in the car. I watched my dad cram all the bags of our stuff into the trunk and back seat, and then he put Tammy and me in the front seat smashed in between him and grandmother.

After we pulled out onto the highway, my grandmother broke the silence. In a loud, irritated voice she exclaimed, "Just tell 'em, Steve!"

Then, my dad's voice broke a little when he said, "Girls, your mom died in a car accident this morning." It was then, the wailing screams began.

When the last sound of her voice ended, no one could breathe. Karen had no emotion the entire time. John had his hands clasped in his lap, stretching his back, trying to hide that he was holding back tears. Rob sat still, looking at Karen with tears down both sides of his face while Ryan was looking out the window. Mary just sat there in a daze like she was in the front seat of the car with Karen.

Karen's eyes locked on to Rob's. Then she spoke, "You see, other people are upset and sad about this, and it seems like I don't even give a damn. I don't feel anything and never have. I just had to pick up and go on. After we drove away, there was no time for crying or feeling anything."

Rob softly responded, "Well, it's ok right now. This is a huge story you have written to share with us. I can't begin to imagine how hard this was, and being so young. All I can ask is that you be patient and open, and let's see where this goes."

A moment passed, then Angela spoke, "You smiled when you shared about the Silver Dollar Pancakes."

Karen decided to engage, "Yeah, that's what I did. Those were my favorite to make. I was used to making breakfast for Tammy, Mom, and me. That was part of my job. But that morning, those people showed up at the door, and it really pissed me off. We had never seen those people before, and there they stood looking lost. I don't even know why the hell they were there. I would guess my aunt sent them over. I suppose they meant well."

There were other questions, and Karen responded with short answers or yes and no as though she wanted to move on.

As time was coming to a close, and they had seemed to not help with anything, Ryan finally spoke with a look of curiosity, "Tell us about your grandmother who was sitting and wringing her hands."

She replied, "Oh, my mom's mom. Lilly was in her seventies, and she was a worrywart and a hypochondriac. She talked about how she was going to die of something almost every day. She had arthritis really bad though. Now, my other grandma, my dad's mom was Katherine. Me and Tammy called her Mimi. She was in the car. That was good because she knew how to take care of us."

John questioned, "What do you mean, take care of you?"

"Well, after we left my mom's that day, dad didn't want us. He was remarried and had other kids, so we went and lived with Mimi again." The first time the name Mimi came out of Karen's mouth, she sat up straight, smiling from ear to ear and talking with her hands. Her face lit up the entire room. She didn't stop. She was like a different person.

"...So that was for three years, but we had lived with Mimi before we moved to Strawberry Plains. Mom had gone through a really rough patch, so we lived with Mimi for about two years until mom could get her own place."

It was as if Karen had gone into another world sharing with us about Mimi. She taught them how to sew and make their own clothes, cook, do laundry, and how to fight off boys if they needed to. Karen also glowed talking about how the three of them loved working in the garden together. She got animated, looking like a baseball pitcher while telling a story about the time they got into a hilarious rotten tomato throwing fight. Sitting straight up with a shine on her face she paused and said, "I suppose she taught us most everything we needed to know about life. Really, all my best childhood memories were when we lived with Mimi."

Everyone knew something special had just taken place but wasn't sure what.

Rob said, "So, it sounds like Mimi was more like a mom for you?"

Karen, with a bit of shock and unsettling acceptance, acknowledged, "Yeah, I suppose she was."

A sacred silence fell.

The Sunroom

"Well, Karen and everyone, I'm sorry, but it's time to transition now." Rob turned to look right at Karen, "Karen, you have done very well. You are getting somewhere with this story. It might not be what you have been looking for, but you are making very important progress. This is good."

Karen said, "Thanks." After glancing at each person in the group, she put her story on the floor. As Karen sat there now done with her turn, she knew that something had changed. She was relieved, scared, but also excited. She felt like she was standing on the edge of something. She didn't know what all this meant, but for sure there was something stirring inside she had never felt before. Hope.

Ryan - "The Pinewood Derby"

Ryan was the only one left. "Well, I wasn't sure what to write, and this seems kind of silly, but it's what I wrote so here goes," he said. The front two legs of his chair came back to the floor as he pulled out his folded up story from his back pocket. Facing toward the floor with his elbows on his knees, he began to read, "This is 'The Pinewood Derby.'"

Growing up, my brother, Brian and I loved to do everything together. We often found ourselves playing Legos and make-believe. When we were eight, my mom thought it would be a good idea to get us involved in Cub Scouts. She thought that our creativity with Legos could be well applied to the things learned in Scouts. From the very start we were building things like bird houses and tool boxes. The coolest thing that I looked forward to was the construction of our Pinewood Derby cars. When the time came, our grandmother helped us cut out the templates to build our cars. The smell of fresh cut wood from the jig-saw was amazing as we followed the pattern laid out on the block of wood provided. It was this block that was going to put us in the winner's circle for the first time ever. After cutting out our cars, we drilled holes for

the wheels, inserted the axles, and painted the cars. I always painted my creations orange, and my brother blue. We wanted everyone to know they were our favorite colors.

Finally the day of the race came, and my mom, grandma, brother, and I loaded up the Toyota Camry and headed off. Arriving, we walked into a room where the wooden slot track was set up in the middle. The room was fairly dim and a little stuffy since so many people were there. We very quickly started to notice that all the other cars didn't look like ours. They had similar shapes, but theirs had well rounded edges and smooth glossy paint jobs.

Car after car went racing down the track. From start to finish, they never missed a second's delay as they gained speed and zoomed across the finish line. Then I heard my name called. When I walked up to the track with the other three boys, their dads were there with them checking wheels, making sure weights were in the right place, and giving a pep talk to their sons. But for me, I was alone with my ordinary car and without a pep talk. Nonetheless, it was time to race. The four of us set our cars on the top and stepped to the side. The gate dropped, and the cars went zooming down the track. All of them, except one. Hearing laughter and snickering, I walked up and picked up my car from where it had stopped in the middle of the track.

One man walked up and said, "Didn't your dad use graphite on the axles?"

As an eight-year-old boy, I replied, "No, Sir. My Grandma helped me build it." Already feeling defeated, I realized that it was quite clear that I was beaten in more ways than one. I couldn't wait to get back home. So we all drove home early.

Brian and I went downstairs and began playing Legos and pretending that everything was normal.

Ryan finished, relieved as if it was all over, but there the group sat with the elephant in the room. Karen started thinking about her own grandma teaching them to use a saw, and Mary reflected on when she quit Brownie's after her group continued to poke fun at her for only selling four boxes of cookies. John had a quiver in his stomach wondering, "Where is his dad? Or does he not have one."

"Ryan, why this particular story?" Rob asked.

"Well, this was one that I long forgot, but as I look back things were never the same after that. I mean, I eventually quit Scouts and started playing soccer which is fine, but this one I've not been able to forget. Also, I've been dating Christine, a nurse for almost three years, but can't bring myself to ask her to marry me, which is crazy. She's amazing. I don't know what's wrong with me. She wants kids, and I'm not ready. It's just too much pressure." Ryan spoke with a bit of a puzzled look.

Karen came out with it, "So, what happened to your dad?"

Ryan responded, "My brother and I are twins, and our dad left us when we were two. Brian and Ryan, right... Anyway, he left us for another woman, and grandma moved in. Then, when I was five, he moved to New York. I didn't see him again until I was twenty."

Mary said, "That's so sad. He really missed out."

"Yeah, he did," Ryan replied.

John spoke, "What was it like seeing him when you were twenty?"

"Well, it was my grandma's funeral of all places. When I looked up, I knew it was him and that tramp he ended up marrying. There was part of me that wanted to punch his lights out." As Ryan spoke, he looked off out the window. "But then, I also wanted to go over and shake his hand and say, 'Hi Dad.' But, I didn't. I just went on like he wasn't there."

There were a few other questions from the group and within a few minutes it seemed like Ryan was wanting to head to the finish line. Just before closing, Mary still had something stirring she couldn't put her finger on. "You mentioned your relationship with Christine being stuck. She wants to have kids and you're not ready. Frankly, I don't know what you are like outside of here, but as far as I can tell, as I think about it, if there was anyone here I'd trust with my kids, it's you, and I don't trust anyone with my kids."

Ryan was shocked and stared right at Mary. "Why is that?" he asked.

"Well, you know more than anyone the true value of kids needing a dad since you didn't have one. You would surely be the best dad ever."

Ryan was frozen. He knew Mary was right. He had dreamed much about what he would do if he was a dad but would never bring himself to speak about it from such gripping fear. Sitting here with this group, he knew it was now out in the open. Ryan said, "Maybe you're right."

John spoke up, "I agree with Mary."

"Me too," Karen agreed.

Rob spoke, "We have come to an end of our time, but there is something I'd like to share with you. I have never shared about a story of mine during someone else's before, but I just can't help it. Oddly enough Ryan, I was in Boy Scouts and loved the Pinewood Derby, too. So did my dad. But, here is the deal. I don't think very many boys actually built their cars. When my dad and I worked on it, he pretty much had me watch. I remember my Uncle Dave had a machine shop, and we went there one night for three hours. I sat on a bench most of the time waiting while he and Dad made Tungsten Carbide axles and countersunk weights to make it perfectly balanced. I liked saying Tungsten Carbide. That's funny." Ryan grinned as Rob went on. "Anyway, Uncle Dave also had this belt sander to make it super slick smooth. Dad did let me hold it while he sanded the body. I got to put on the sticker numbers. That was the only thing I really did. My car came in second, and I got a trophy to put on my shelf. Dad was really proud. As I look back, that's pretty much what everyone did." Rob picked up and opened a zipper pouch. "I even have a picture of me and my dad holding my car and trophy right here. Check this out."

Ryan looked at the picture and even in the Polaroid you could tell it was more his dad's car and trophy than his. Rob finished, "Actually, the trophy didn't mean much. A couple years later, we moved, and I threw it away. At least you got to build your own car."

Ryan quietly whispered, "Yeah, I sure did."

Then everyone said, "Thanks, Ryan."

The Deck

F rancie loved the outdoors. Some of the group was surprised that it was still cold out, but there was an unspoken feeling of it being fun to follow the farm girl outside. Francie said, "Ok, here we go. Bundle up if you need to and grab a blanket. It's so beautiful; we're going out."

This was awesome for Brock with his farmer jeans, flannel shirt, and boots already on. It also sounded good to Lisa as she loved to curl up in a blanket at home and watch Netflix. Angela and Greg both were just needing to be told what to do, and it didn't matter where they met. Nothing was going to change the fact they had to share their stories in front of people.

As Brock stepped out to the deck, he was excited but his head was spinning at the same time. Writing his story at the last minute and the fact he would be in a group with women, seemed to escape his mind until group members were announced. He felt great about everyone until the last name of his group was called...Angela. There was something about her that made him convinced she didn't like him.

Brock

When he arrived on Friday, he climbed out of his dirt covered, squeaky door pick-up truck, had on worn-out jeans, a t-shirt, a go-tee, and was smoking a Marlboro Red. He had driven twelve hours to get here. Most people complain about driving across town. Where he lived, it was a twenty-minute drive to the next stop sign and an hour drive to go out to eat in Guymon, Oklahoma.

Being a farmer, Brock's life had been seasonal for fifty years. After attending a men's only retreat last year, he had hoped the weather would make a way for him to come to this one, and the rain came. Upon meeting Brock, no one would have guessed he farmed ten thousand acres,

The Deck

was a board member for two multi-billion dollar companies, and had just gotten off his cracked cell phone trading $75,000 of technology stock.

The first twenty years of marriage, Brock read dozens of Christian books, went to Promise Keepers twice, attended three men's leadership conferences, and led The Purpose Driven Life series at church. But after his wife, Joanne, discovered his pornography addiction, she and the kids left him on the farm alone. Now, Joanne is remarried, he has weekend visitation with his kids, and his dad's slow death has left him to run the farm by himself. Brock long ago boxed up his Christian books, and his quiet time he spent with a Bible was traded for quiet time with a bottle.

The first retreat, Brock had explored a story he called, "Asleep at the Wheel." At the age of 12, he had been driving one of the combines for sixteen hours on a Saturday, fell asleep, and wrecked into the grain collection truck. His dad came and yelled at him for being so "stupid." He had been beat down like that since he could remember and has lived with the daily anxiety of making mistakes. Six weeks after that retreat, he was doing better than he could ever remember. Then one wild night out cost him a DWI and has now left him a millionaire farmer with a restricted driver's license.

From the age of six, besides two winter months and during school hours, Brock worked the farm with his dad, even into the night with lights on the tractors. Every year on the 4th of July, he would watch the fireworks twenty miles away from the cab of a tractor. His five sisters and all his friends would be in town having fun. His dad would say, "Son, this is a time provided by God for us to get ahead of everyone else. We need to get it while the gettin's good."

With the urging of his mom and not his dad, he was allowed to go to college. He was shocked to find that he was quite intelligent and a good bit ahead of his class. His junior year, he and two professors worked on a research project that made him a patent holder and landed him in Washington, DC doing a presentation at the US Department of Agriculture. Several large technology firms made him job offers before his senior year even began.

It was the beginning of his senior year that he met Joanne while moving in to his apartment. By Christmas they were engaged, married in March, and pregnant in April. A week before final exams, Brock accepted a job in DC working for a contract technology firm for double the average starting pay of his peers.

It was the following Monday, just before his statistics final, that he got the long-distance call. "Brock, it's your dad. I'm afraid that I am falling ill. A serious ill, maybe from the war, and won't be able to farm anymore. The Schoffner legacy and family name is at risk. I really need you to come run the farm until I start feeling better, or we could lose everything."

While they were engaged, Joanne made Brock promise they would never go back to the farm. With ten thousand acres and the family name on the line, he told Joanne that it would only be for one year. As his dad's health, slowly improved, so did his dad's desire to build a bigger empire, and before long, he had Brock investing in the farm by signing loans to buy land and more equipment. His dad would often say at the end of a hard day's work, "Brock, one day the farm will all be yours." One year turned to three, three to seven. Then the markets dropped, and by the seventh year, Brock had accumulated $800,000 in debt. There was no way to get out but to keep farming and put in as many hours as possible. For Joanne, it was one broken promise after another. And every hope and dream that would come in the spring would soon die after every fall harvest on his dad's farm.

His parents are both eighty-six and in a nursing home sixty miles away, Brock is still working the family farm, and his dad checks on him every day. Brock is now fifty-five.

Lisa

It was not easy for Lisa to be the youngest of four and a PK, preacher's kid. Her dad was from Colorado, and her mom was from the Philippines. They had met on a mission trip and a year later were married. Lisa was born in

The Deck

Indiana, and new churches took her family to South Carolina, Ohio, then to Alabama, and finally Denver, Colorado. Growing up, Lisa had endless possibilities and options. Being the daughter of the lead pastor who was also the headmaster of the school, seven days a week, she could do anything she wanted…. as long as it was related to their church.

Lisa is twenty-six now and rents a small, remodeled home on the south side of the city. On Sunday mornings, as she gets in her car for church, she often sees her neighbors out on their front porches. She would shake her head as she got behind the wheel, unable to imagine what it might be like to miss church. For Lisa, ChristianMingle.com has been a source for her belief of not being compatible with any man and fuels her feelings of despair.

Two years ago, not sure what to do next with her life, she decided to get her MBA at nights while she worked as a wedding planner at a well-to-do boutique on the west side of town. It's been a grueling struggle to see almost a hundred weddings pass through the doors of 'Now and Forever.' For herself, she refers to it as, "No Not Ever." The woman who owns the place is sixty years old, bitter, and divorced. It also doesn't help that her two male co-workers are privately dating each other. Lisa has had to hear the story a dozen times of how they met online last January and in March discovered they worked at the same place.

It is the dreams of her own wedding that makes her one of the most gifted and desired planners in town and the only one close to her age. She finished her master's this past December, but no one seemed to notice and nothing changed except the amount of her college loan repayment plan. Coming here was the first time she flew on a plane. Walking through Chicago's O'Hare International Airport, she felt the typical awareness of being unnoticed and insignificant. Lisa wakes up every morning, hoping the day will bring something different, very different. Especially today.

Greg

At the age of six, Greg was at school in the cafeteria. He was trying to make new friends, and a few of the other boys invited him to join their club. They eventually called him stupid for thinking he could be in their club and threw green beans in the cafeteria. Greg got in trouble for 'horsing around,' the lunch monitor called it. The school called his mom to come and pick him up at the end of the day from the principal's office. Greg didn't speak in the principal's office or all the way home. When they arrived home, Greg went straight to his bedroom closet with a Piggly Wiggly paper sack and began packing it. One favorite shirt, jeans, five socks, two pairs of underwear, his pocket-knife, and $2.35. He decided he would carry his fishing pole from the garage in the other hand. He grabbed the paper handles of the paper sack, walked down the hall, out the front door, and stood on the front step. His mom saw him just as he walked out and went to him. "Greg, where are you going?" she asked.

"I'm running away from this town. No one likes me, so I am leaving here, and I'm not coming back," he responded.

His mom continued, "But this is your home. You live here."

Greg snapped, "This is not my home. This is not where I'm supposed to live. I'm supposed to live in Illinois."

He was right. His parents had divorced in Illinois a year earlier, and his mom had married another man who lived in Iowa. This wouldn't be the last time Greg felt homeless. Over the next twelve years, Greg's mom would be divorced and married again, and his dad would move away from Illinois after marrying a woman in Nebraska.

Greg met Mary while he was in trade school in Chicago. They were smitten with each other and got married just after he got his electrical contractor's license. Working for a union in Chicago, Greg still gets frustrated that he took a 50% cut in pay when they moved to Nashville. But Mary wanted to live close to family after her mom's close call with cancer. About twice a

The Deck

year, Greg, Mary, and the kids go to holidays and family reunions of previous step-parents that were Greg's favorites when he grew up.

Greg would never want Mary to know, but 'home' is the one place he feels most uncomfortable, as if he should be somewhere else. He often works late or takes projects out of town. Mary has concluded Greg's distance is because of her.

Angela

The past four years have been a blur for Angela. Even though she knew leaving her abusive husband was best, nothing could have prepared her for the grief, loneliness, and impossible role of a single mom left with three teenagers still at home. This weekend would have been her 20th anniversary. Their marriage was fairly empty and dry with her husband, Paul, daily focused on building his surgical device company, MGI. But the income, having a companion and a whole family, kept a spring in her step most days.

She has worked as a home caregiver, nurse for the elderly the past ten years. For too many years to count, Paul said his business was going to take off. Then the drinking started, periodically at first, but then it became every day. As Paul's condition worsened, so did MGI's. Angela confronted Paul several times and became frightened of him and his rage. The last year of their marriage, Paul continued to work every day and then began to work "remotely" with scotch at home. He would never speak of him having a drinking problem to Angela, the kids, or anyone. It was an unspoken rule that it would not be discussed. There had been many rules like that over the years, and finally, Angela took the girls to her mom's and was divorced four months later.

Two years after the divorce, with the encouragement of her youngest daughter, Josie, she signed up for a speed dating night downtown. After two intense hours, she was interested in none of the twenty-five men but got back a sheet where seven of them were interested in her. She didn't know how that was possible.

The Deck

Then came Christmas. It was the second Christmas without a man, father, or husband. It seemed like a bigger hole in their home than ever before. On Christmas Eve while the family was making cookies in the kitchen, Angela walked upstairs to her room, grabbed a pillow off her bed, walked into the closet, got down on the floor, and cried in her pillow. Then, Josie yelled upstairs for her. She stood up and went to the bathroom to wash

her face. As she looked in the mirror, she said to herself, "Oh God, I can't be alone anymore."

With her eyes and heart open, she began to go to the gym, bought new clothes, and experimented with makeup her best friend, Jamie, bought for her. By February, she met James. They had met at the home of Ms. Hendry, who was 92. James was her grandson and would stop to visit on Wednesday's during his lunch break whenever he could. He was divorced with no kids, and one day while they both were at Ms. Hendry's, he gave Angela his business card and said with a soft smile, "If you ever need anything, don't hesitate to give me a call." Ten days later, they went on their first date.

Angela had a new spring in her step during those first few months. Talking about life with a man who was interesting and found her interesting was rich. The first movie date they had, after an hour, James put his left arm on top of the back of her seat and with his right, gently took hold of her hand. Her heart and mind raced with a deep breath as she had not been touched by a man in almost three years. After the movie, they even held hands down the sidewalk to the ice cream shop. Heading home that night, she felt a hope that was like a strong wind in her sails after being stranded in the middle of the ocean since she was small.

Six more months of dating and things began to change between them. A distance grew. Approaching one year, James seemed to pull away. It was Angela that would take his hand now. Angela also struggled with the physical part of their relationship. Anything heavier than kissing made her feel awkward. She had an overwhelming desire and, at the same time, felt dirty. She knew that getting married wasn't the answer to this paradox as she had the same feelings in her marriage to Paul. Two weeks before their one-year anniversary, at the same restaurant as their first date, James let Angela know he'd decided it was best for them to be friends.

At forty-four now, her oldest son, Andy is getting married in two months, and she carries the burden of having no money for the rehearsal dinner. She has been fighting depression for a thousand days.

The Deck

Angela's life goals are to live out her days, be the best mom she can, serve people at work, and pay off her home before she dies. Being with Francie as her facilitator was a relief, but she really didn't care who else was in her group. However, when Lisa stood up from the couch to prepare to go outside, Angela got discouraged because she was confident that Lisa was so young she simply wouldn't be able to relate.

Rocking Chairs

The sun was too bright to sit in the field or around the fire pit, so Francie picked the corner nook of the wrap-around deck. Everyone grabbed one of the solid oak rocking chairs and put them in a circle. Greg sat straight up in his seat with his eyes wide open. Lisa wrapped herself completely in a blanket before she sat down, and Angela was bundled up, hiding inside her coat and seemingly half withdrawn from everyone. Brock appeared excited with his worn out boot propped up on his knee. Francie rocked back and forth with a big smile and said, "Well, guess what? Everyone is going to go eventually. Would anyone like to start us off?"

"Sure," Brock said. His excitement on the outside became a churning stomach on the inside. If there was any time he needed a cigarette, it was right now. "All right, so here we go."

Brock - "Lost in the Hayloft"

It was a hot summer Saturday with the expectation of having some fun with no school. My favorite thing to do in 7th grade was to ride motorcycles with my two friends, Greg and John. We usually rode southwest of Glaser along the creek near an old railroad bridge. Our motorcycle trails we called the "railroad trestle."

This day, however, I rode with a different friend named Mark. We had gone to church since I was five, and he was eight. Mark was crazier than me and did the riskiest things his mind could conjure up. Now, for sure, Mark at fifteen and me twelve, he was always the leader, and I was the follower.

I drove over to his house on my gold, Honda SL 125 motorcycle. Then we piggy backed to my house, so he could jump on my blue Honda CB 125. We took off and cruised east and then north out of town to State Highway 35. We went a few miles east and pulled out into the pasture where his show lambs were kept. We shut down for a few minutes while he checked the water and fed his lambs. Off in the distance, down along the creek were a few cottonwood trees and an old barn. "Hey, Brock! I want to show you something," said Mark. He fired up his motorcycle, and I followed him. We rode through the pasture, pulled in to the old barn, and took off our helmets. There was a ladder against the wall, and Mark climbed up first. After following him up, it was dim inside, and as my eyes adjusted, I was amazed to discover on the floor stacks and stacks of porn magazines. There were several hundred magazines in all. It was like a lightning bolt to my brain as my excitement sky rocketed. I had found the goldmine!

Mark rifled through a few and sat down on the far side and began to look through them. I started looking through the stacks of magazines and grabbed a few. It didn't take long to realize these were not the normal, torn up Playboys we were used to finding along the road. My excitement was off the charts as I looked thru them and saw men and women doing wild things. I sat down on the other side of the loft and began to flip page after page. I had never seen stuff like this or even knew it existed. I settled into reading a story about a British man and woman. I was in my own little world for sure as I imagined the scenes in the magazines. I was more excited than I had ever been.

A few minutes later, Mark held up a magazine in his left hand and started talking to the picture like he was a stud or something. I wanted to go back into the story I had been reading but couldn't help but listen and watch Mark. He eventually stopped and seemed to have some sense of deep satisfaction. I went back to reading. I wanted to stay there forever and look at every one of those magazines. I started to gather up a few magazines to take with me when Mark said with an angry look on his face, "Put them back. These are not yours. Let's go!" He climbed down first, and as I went down, I looked at the stacks with longing and wanting to see more. Then we got back on our motorcycles.

When Brock had begun to read his story, Greg could almost feel the wind in his hair, and Lisa imagined petting the lambs. But everyone knew this story was not leading to smelling daisies. Angela knew a story like this all too well and where it was headed. She had a girlfriend like Mark when she was only ten. In Brock's story, by the time he was climbing down the ladder, Angela could not hold back tears and tried to wipe them away before anyone could see. Lisa was tense the whole time, and by the end, her mind was bouncing like a ping-pong ball, and her hands were cold and sweaty.

Greg was in shock and awe that a man would share a story like this in front of women. He thought, "Well, now it's out there. Brock has just exposed every man in the world, including me, to these women. This will be interesting."

Francie said, "Wow, Brock. I am so amazed by your courage to bring this story to our group." Those few words gave Brock such relief. It was as though he had been holding his breath the whole time he read it. The look on Francie's face reminded Brock of his favorite elementary school teacher, Ms. Jackson, who told him once, "Brock, one day, you will change the world." No one had ever spoke anything like that to him or ever had since. After looking at Francie, Brock took a quick glance at the others and noticed Angela's tears and a warm, soft look of compassion on Lisa's face. He was convinced the women would scowl, condemn him, or at least be silently angry. Their response of acceptance and compassion was overwhelming. Tears began to fall as he spoke softly, "My wife left me after catching me looking at porn. The divorce was very public, and she turned all my daughters against me, too. It took a year before my youngest daughter, Jessie, would speak to me. During the court proceedings, Joanne brought up every accusation you can imagine and even tried to have me committed to a sex addict recovery program in Arizona. I've never been able to get her words out of my head, "You are a f****ing freak, and I am going to ruin you." When he said those haunting words out loud, it was as if he was playing a recording. The word 'freak' struck a chord with everyone in the circle.

It was tempting for group members to ask about his divorce, daughters, and other troubles, but the elephant was out in the open. Angela spoke up, "I must admit, I am honored that you would trust us, and it's an honor to sit in the hayloft with you."

"Absolutely," Lisa said in agreement.

Greg spoke up, "Yeah. Agreed."

When Brock heard Angela refer to sitting in the hayloft, he began to squirm in his seat.

The ladies asked several questions about guilt and shame, and finally Greg spoke. "Brock, I am so sorry this happened to you. This sucks. Was it just this one time?"

Brock responded, "No, we went back quite a few times over that year. It all stirred me up. I felt like I was finally in on the big secret that no one was telling me."

Lisa asked, "So had your parents explained anything to you about sex?"

"No, my parents never told me anything about sex. In fact, I never knew if my parents even had sex themselves. I'm sure they did, but they were very private. They didn't even hold hands or hug at home or in public. My dad wasn't touchy feely like that. Finally, when I was seventeen after the final harvest, my dad told me that he wanted to talk with me on the porch about something really important in being a man. I was so excited. We got showered; he got out two beers and gave me one. It was our first beer together. Even though I'd already had sex with a girl, I knew this was the talk I'd been waiting for." Brock's face lit up as he shared with the group. "Dad said a few things. He was nervous. Then he said, 'Brock, there is something you need to know that's really important I learned a long, long time ago. No matter where life takes you, keep your dick out of the payroll.' Leaning back in his rocking chair, Brock began to get angry as he continued, "That was it. That's all he had to say. Don't have sex with women at work. What the hell was that supposed to mean? That's what I got from my dad. A year later, a week before I left for college, my mom left a pamphlet on my bed. It said on the front, 'Masturbation - A Natural Part of Life.' Once again, I'd already been having sex, and this was my education. Whoopee."

Lisa asked, "So you said in your story, 'these weren't like the Playboys we would find on the side of the road.' What were they?"

Brock's eyes got big along with a lump in his throat as his mind scrambled to come up with an answer to this question. He didn't have time to make up a lie, so he decided to continue rolling with the honest approach. "Well, there were different kinds of men and women, women and women, and even men and men having sex in all kinds of situations and stuff like that. Other guys seemed to like the pictures, but I liked to read the stories. I'm not sure why. It was crazy but intoxicating at the same time. I came to believe that this is what it meant to be a real man. But, I was a nerd, didn't play sports, and girls were not interested in me. I was a loner. Then I went to college, that all changed. I became the life of the party, and girls liked me, but sometimes I partied too much. Then I met Joanne and brought all that crap into our marriage. I didn't know how to treat a woman. She deserved so much better," he said as tears began to drip to his beard.
The group was silent for a long time while Brock sat there crying. They all knew the tears had been stored up for many years. Each one was like a diamond.

After a while, Francie asked, "Have you told anyone this story before?"

Rocking Chairs

He answered, "No. This has caused me so much trouble and pain in my life. After being married for years, Mark was even in my Sunday school class. Joanne would have him and his wife over for dinner. We never talked about it. To be honest with you...this morning, I totally lost track of time when we were supposed to be writing our story. I didn't know what story to pick, and then this came to me. I wrote it in ten minutes and didn't think much about it. Then, when groups were announced, it occurred to me I would be in a co-ed group and began to panic." They all chuckled along with Brock, and he went on. "I thought, how can I quickly write a different story. But then I thought, "Oh well, this must be the story I'm supposed to have."

Time was coming to a close as Francie spoke, "I know I'm a woman, but I do know there is more to being a man than his sexuality. One of the most important characteristics of a man is being courageous and willing to head into battle in times of conflict and war. Brock, that is exactly what we have all seen you do in front of us. I am so glad you're here because we need a warrior to lead us into battle. You are a brave man." As her eyes sparkled with a big smile, Brock stopped breathing for a long while to take in the moment, trying to burn those words into his mind.

Brock had been waiting for forty-three years for someone to climb up the hayloft ladder and help him. Never in a million years did he think it would be a strange man and three women in the Smoky Mountains.

Lisa - "Moving"

The group sat there silently waiting to see what Francie would do next. Lisa could feel it. All eyes seemed to drift to her. Then she said with a smile, "I'm going to have to go eventually, so let's do it. This is probably just a silly story, but when Francie said that it could be a story that has bothered you for a long time, this is what I decided. So here goes. 'Moving.'"

Having lived in Warsaw, Indiana for two years, I was comfortable with my family, our church and school, my friends, and where I was growing up. Most of my time was spent at church, which was also my school, since my dad was lead pastor and principal, and my mom was Children's Director and teacher. The faint smell of wood from the pews and old carpet from the most used aisle down the middle would embrace me as I entered the sanctuary. I was comfortable roaming in and out of the church building, to the Sunday school classes, and over to the gym which had school classes all around. It was the beginning of summer when I was nine-years-old, and my parents had just told the congregation we were moving to Fort Myers, Florida. They said it would be a new and exciting adventure for us again.

After service, the whole congregation went over to the gym to fellowship and have a pot luck, which we did at least once a month. Like kids would do, me and my friends rushed eating whatever our moms put on our plate so we could go play. We would run and chase each other, playing a game of tag because kickball wasn't allowed with so many people in the gym. We were playing and getting winded when my best friend Catherine pulled me aside into the alcove where the outside door would lead to the path to the church.

It was dark and gloomy in the hallway. I faced towards the gym, and she was facing the door. Bathrooms and water fountain were to my right and hooks for jackets and purses were to my left. All of a sudden, she began to cry. She told me, "I am so sad you are leaving and moving away from me." I was so surprised that she was upset. I didn't know what to say. I wasn't expecting this reaction. Once she stopped talking, she put her head in her hands, and her shoulders began to shake from the force of her tears. I stood there frozen.

I noticed from behind her someone started to walk our way. I looked up, and my brother, Jimmy, walked over to us, put his arm around my shoulder, and asked if we were ok. I nodded my head, and that's when I felt them on my cheeks. I began crying just as much as Catherine. I didn't understand why I was crying. I don't remember starting to cry or feeling the lump of emotion in my throat that I usually would when I cried. I was unsure of these new feelings. Moving would be an adventure; moving was not unusual in my family. We were just going to another place; it wasn't like I would never talk to her again. But as all three of us stood there, my brother's arm around my shoulder, me silently crying, and my friend with her face in her hands, I knew this was altogether different than before.

Everyone knew this was a significant story and had compassion for Lisa as she sat there confused even now with tears. Angela felt the pain of love lost. Greg knew the trauma of moving but without a whole family. Brock, with his boots planted on the deck floor and leaning in closely to listen, could remember several times sitting in his sisters' rooms while they cried when friends moved away. Francie had gone to four different high schools because of her parents' divorce. At the age of forty-four, she still felt the heartache of losing friends and that moving was not an exciting adventure for a child.

Lisa spoke, "You see, Francie, even now I have tears running down my face, and I don't even know why. This seems like a silly story compared to other ones. I have other stories like my dog dying in my arms, getting lost at the zoo, and a story about an older cousin, but this one bugs me even worse."

Lisa was really upset that this was so troubling. Angela was caught off guard about her older cousin comment, and Greg got worked up after imagining what it would be like if his daughter got lost at the zoo. Brock had a soft smile, knowing there was more to Lisa than even what Lisa knew.

Francie began, "Alright Lisa, this is a really good story to bring, and it is clearly important. Frankly, I think it's apparent to all of us how significant this story is." Everyone shook their heads in agreement.

Francie invited Lisa to go further, "You seem really surprised about Catherine being upset you were moving away, so can you tell us more about her?"

"Sure. We were definitely pretty close. We went to school and church together. We even went on vacation together at the beginning of that summer. I think we went to Charleston, South Carolina. Yes, that's right. I'd never been on vacation with someone else before."

Brock spoke, "Going on vacation is a pretty big deal for a nine-year-old. Did your family go?"

"No, I went with Catherine's family. We all were close since we lived in the basement of Catherine's house. We couldn't afford a regular home, so her mom and dad fixed up their basement for us."

Angela remarked, "So she was like a sister to you?"

Lisa responded with a curious glance toward the cow pasture. "Well, my own sister was five years older than me. She was busy doing older things. Catherine was like my sister, and my same age."

Angela continued, "So there wasn't anything you two didn't do together."

"No, we pretty much did everything together. Her bedroom was right above mine. We had sleepovers all the time."

Brock spoke up, "It sounds like to me that you were the sister Catherine always dreamed of. I'll be honest with you, Lisa. Since I got here, you've been so kind to me and other people, too. You listen to people, and frankly last night after dinner, you asked me what it was like to be a farmer. I've never had anyone ask me that. Having to answer that question, I went from being somewhat embarrassed and feeling like an outsider to feeling proud to be a farmer. I've only been around you for a few hours, and it's clear to me why Catherine was so sad. You made her feel loved; like she was important." Lisa's eyes were open wide as she listened.

With a gentle smile, Angela commented, "I didn't even know you were going to be in my group, and out of the blue at breakfast, you sat down right next to me in front of the fire like we'd been friends forever. It was actually really nice. Oddly enough, if you left right now, I'm sure I would miss you."

Then Lisa responded to a question from Greg about growing up a pastor's kid and her favorite place to live, but after a while she sat there quietly. "Now, thinking about it, after moving from Indiana, that's when I stopped getting close to anyone. And that's still my problem. Even dating gives me anxiety. Who knows if the guy will even be around in six months," she said.

Greg exhaled and thought what all the others were thinking, "Wow, so this is how someone awesome can end up still single at the age of twenty-six."

They explored some about her favorite place to live and other friendships over the years, then Francie said, "Lisa, we're going to have to begin to transition now, but you have made some real progress. Before we end, there is one critical piece that I want you to hear that may be of help. Are you ready?"

"Yep." she said as she sat up straight.

Francie continued, "Much research has shown that for a child, especially between 8 and 12, moving is the most common traumatic childhood event after death and divorce. If you think about it, all at once, most everything you have ever known changes: your relationships, activities, school, bedroom, kitchen, streets and sidewalks, down to the sounds, to even where you put your toothbrush. That has a major impact on a child. That's just one. In your story, you even said, 'Moving was not unusual,' so that means, the trauma of moving was normal. For an adult, moving is hard, but by the time you are older, you are more equipped to handle changes in life."

For Lisa and the others, it was as though a cloud of lifelong confusion lifted about this. As it sank in, Lisa thought to herself, "Wow, maybe I'm not a freak for this bothering me so much."

"Hopefully, that's helpful, so you can quit beating yourself up about this bothering you. This is huge in your life."

"Yeah, I see that, for sure now," Lisa responded.

Francie finished with a challenge. "Now, here is my challenge for you to consider. Are you willing to take the risk of the joy of connection while knowing that it won't last? Are you willing to take in however long you do have?" Looking right in Lisa's eyes, Francie said, "You've done well. Good job, Lisa."

Lisa smiled along with everyone else.

Greg - "Bicycle 911"

It was now between Greg and Angela. Greg didn't care if he went next, but Angela had hoped to go last from the beginning, so she sat quiet with her written story under her rocking chair. That made it obvious to Greg it was his turn. "Well, I would say here goes nothin', but I suppose Francie wouldn't like that." Everyone chuckled. "It's called, 'Bicycle 911.' Greg sat up, stretched, and got in just the right posture as to read the group a masterpiece. Hearing the title alone, it was clear that it was about a bike. Lisa loved bikes, Angela hated them, and Brock felt a bit aloof as growing up on a ten-thousand-acre farm, bikes were of no use. He skipped right to motorcycles and tractors by age four. Brock, in his head, could hear his dad saying, "There's no time to play games." Then Greg began reading.

 *It's a hot summer's Saturday after starting eighth grade; My M.O. is staying inside bound to my room, listening to my "prize" stereo system. The school season had just begun, and I was not at all excited about returning to this abusive prison for another year. Saturdays were mostly boring for me as I had no close friends or places to go. I did have a couple friendly kids in my neighborhood who would talk to me (outside of school), but there seemed to be a silent unspoken agreement to never let anyone at school know.*

I wanted to go for a ride on my bike but needed a destination, otherwise, what would be the point. I knew of a boy nearby, TJ Greene, who was harassed and neglected at school. One of the lowly types, an easy target you might say. It would be a quick, easy five block bike ride to his house to see if he'd like to play. I confirmed with my parents, retrieved my bike from our super cluttered garage, but I forgot that the front tire was still bent from a bike accident. Dad was always sure to tell us exactly how much money we didn't have at every meal at the dinner table, so we weren't able to fix my bike yet. Then, I looked over and saw my dad's bike, a mountain bike, 18 gears, chromed with red accent. From riding his bike before, I knew the brakes were not that good, so I decided to fix them. I grabbed tools from my dad's tool bench at the front of the garage, removed both tires and chain, greased it up, reassembled the bike, and fixed the brakes.

I'm OFF! Off on a great adventure with a boy I didn't really care to be around, but it was better than staying at home with my family all alone... I zoomed in and out of winding road corners and down roads as fast as I could. One corner in particular, had a dip at the intersection that was fun to whip in and out of.

My visit with TJ was short; we played for only fifteen minutes before he was called inside. Back home would be my new destination. Roughly a block from TJ's house I found a pot hole that was just right to pop a wheelie over! I lifted the front end of the bike as if I was "Evel Knievel." Then, I saw it happen. That moment when you know this isn't going to end well. That very moment when I realized that the front wheel did not lift with the rest of the bike. It was in fact, rolling down the road ahead of me. The bike came down hard on the front forks, sending me soaring over the handlebars and sliding down the road. The world seemed to stop for a second. I was lying on my back trying to put together the pieces in my mind of what just happened. As I tried to lift myself, I was in pain and realized the sting of road rash on my arm was actually, quite a bit worse. I couldn't move my arm, and it was not straight at all. I looked down at my hands and saw them covered in my own blood. I tried again to get up, knowing I was in big trouble for wrecking my dad's bike. I couldn't get up. I tried to flag down two cars. Finally, a white SUV stopped. An older woman and her husband stepped out of the vehicle to check on me. After getting my address, the man sped off to find my house to get my dad. The woman stayed with me. I felt bad for being such an inconvenience. When my dad and stepmom arrived in our station wagon, they propped me up on the tailgate. I apologized for bleeding all over the car. We started hearing a siren in the distance; the man who had gone to get my dad also called 911. The ambulance arrived on the scene, and the paramedics jumped into action. They pulled the bed stretcher out of the back of the ambulance and strapped me down. They strapped down my head, arms and legs. I couldn't move... they were extra careful with my left arm and wrapped it loosely. I was then loaded into the back of the ambulance; the paramedic got into the back with me, the driver got in the driver's seat, and my dad chose to sit in the passenger's seat in the front of the ambulance. I could overhear Dad ranting to the driver, "We can't afford any of this mess. Do you have any idea how much just this ambulance ride costs?" and it went on. Strapped in with tears flowing, I softly said, "Dad, I'm so sorry for wrecking your bike and the cost of all this."

After arriving at the hospital, we waited for hours to be seen. The nurses took me back for x-rays, pulling my arm straight. That pain was worse than the wreck itself. It was a four-hour surgery receiving two metal plates, twelve screws, and two long bolts that would hold my arm together the rest of my life. It was a compound fracture that split my upper arm bone. I was in the hospital for a week. My father didn't speak about it after the surgery or ever again.

Everyone sat there speechless. As Greg was reading, Lisa couldn't help but stare at his arm and think about him having to go through an x-ray machine like she saw at the airport. For Angela, this affirmed her hatred for bikes, and Brock got so mad at Greg's dad that his neck was burning red as he tapped the arms of his chair.

When Greg was done, he sat there in a fog. He was excited about reading the story to everyone because it was a real adventure story, but at the same time he was embarrassed how it all went. He sat there waiting, not knowing what to do next.

Lisa finally spoke, "Greg, I have to say, I am sorry this happened to you."

The words she spoke made Greg start to feel a bit dizzy. For twenty-six years, he had never heard those words he so longed to hear. After a moment he said, "Thanks."

Brock asked about his stereo. Angela asked about his friend TJ. Lisa then brought up the blood on the car and Greg admitted, "I had already created such problems and wrecked Dad's mountain bike, and then to get blood on the car made it even worse."

Lisa's brow began to tighten up, "Let me get this straight. You broke your arms into pieces, bleeding everywhere, people calling an ambulance, and you felt bad about the bike and blood stains?"

Becoming louder as he spoke, Greg lashed out, "Yeah! Because I was stupid! I never should have taken Dad's bike. I was supposed to earn money to fix my own bike. It was all my fault. When I wrecked my own bike, it was from being stupid, too!"

The whole group sank down in their seats. It was like someone else was yelling, "stupid!" Greg said it with such conviction and hostility, it gave everyone chills.

Francie stopped, "Now, wait a minute. That is not being kind. This is a really good story you have brought to the group, but while we explore it, Greg, be kind to yourself. Now Greg, when I grew up, Evel Knievel was a really big deal. It's all everyone talked about at school during the weeks he was going to do a stunt. We had friends who didn't have color TV that came over to watch the night he jumped all those buses. When you were reading your story, I was right there with you. Were you a good rider?"

"Well, I really was. My broken bike was actually my newest BMX. I had won the thirteen to seventeen-year-old BMX race at the county fair, and three days later I ran straight into a curb and crunched my rim. Can you believe that? Stupid. That one hurt pretty bad, but when mom asked me if I got hurt, I told her no. There were bruises all across my waist."

Rocking Chairs

Francie wasn't going to let another "stupid" go by. With a puzzled look, she spoke softly, "Alright, so here we are, again with calling yourself stupid. I realize you made a mistake, but I'd like to get something straight and really think about a couple questions. First, would you say that a thirteen-year-old who beats twenty other racers that are three to four years older is typically someone who is stupid?"

The other group members laser focused on Greg. He thought a long moment and with strong hesitation responded, "I suppose not."

Francie went on, "Just one more question. People who have their electrical contractor's license, are people like that stupid, Greg?"

Greg sat silent.

"How about the rest of you? What do you think? Can stupid people get an electrical contractors license?" A couple of them raised their eyebrows while they all said, "No."

They sat quietly and waited for Greg to respond. He thought about what all it took to get his license and the fact that he's worked on big projects in thirty-nine states. He slowly let it out, "Yeah, I suppose not."

Francie pushed further, "As hard as this is, I must admit, with my experience in life, someone like that has to be pretty smart, and I think it's obvious to the rest of us that you are pretty smart, Greg."

He glanced around and finally right at Francie. "Maybe you're right. Maybe I am smart." Then he looked down. Everyone sat there in silence. Just breathing, they all knew something beyond space and time just happened.

Still looking at Greg, who was in a daze, Francie said, "Yes, you are Greg. You are smart. Now, let's move on."

Angela had been patiently waiting, "So, let me get this straight. You won the county fair at thirteen against seventeen-year-olds?"

"Yep. That's probably why the boys at school didn't like me much," he said with a half grin.

Brock blurted out, "They didn't like you because you were a champion! That's why!"

Greg sat back in his chair and began to breathe deeply, "Yeah, I know."

Lisa asked another question, and then the last question came from Angela. "So what was it like to be the grand champion at the fair?"

As if he were there again, Greg recounted, "It was a dream come true. Ten thirty at night. The final race. Twenty-one bikers, and I was in front. When I jumped the last dirt double in the air, I knew I was the only one out in front. I nailed it and dug the dirt in the final turn and blew across the finish line. The crowd was going nuts. I came back to the line to get the checkered flag and took one more lap. Even most of the other bikers were standing and clapping, but when I came back around to get my trophy, there was only one thing missing to my dream. My dad. He stayed home to work in the garage. I still have the trophy in a box in the attic."

Pausing for just a moment, Francie then spoke, "Greg, you had us all cheering for you in the stands, and we still are. I've got to tell you; your dad just plain missed out. He just missed out a lot. But we're not missing out. We're here right now, and you've definitely been a champion today."

With a tear, Greg replied, "Yes, I am right here. Right now. I sure am."

Francie said, "Thanks, Greg."

Everyone felt a real sense of accomplishment but also that there was more. Everyone knew that Greg hating himself had to be addressed.

Rocking Chairs

Angela - "The Guy Next Door"

Three of the four group members had survived and only one more to go. But, there had been a heaviness in the thick air, and it had not gotten any lighter. In fact, as Angela bent down to get her paper from under her chair, it seemed to weigh a hundred pounds.

"Well, here goes. I suppose I will call this story, 'The Guy Next Door,'" she said.

Brock's stomach sank, and Lisa checked out for a moment. "This can't be good," Greg thought.

 *I crept down the hallway avoiding the creaky spots in the floor, pausing with every few steps to listen and re-assess for sounds of my sleeping parents. I had practiced sneaking out so that I would be ready for this night. Brian, a senior that I met recently, was coming. He was picking up my best friend, Amy, and his best friend, and we were going to cruise together in his car or hang out in the empty house next door. My dad had the key to it hanging in the kitchen, and I slipped it in my pocket.*

I was a sophomore, the end of March, and the night air was crisp. The grass was wet with dew and cold on my feet. I ran across the lawns to the Seven-Eleven parking lot two doors down where they waited. He drove a long, black old car with two doors. The big doors that swung really wide. You had to put the front seat up for passengers to climb into the big bench seat in the back. His car sat idling, no doubt to keep the heat on. I was a little scared about what I was doing but didn't want to disappoint my friend Amy, so I ran up behind the car with gravel crunching under my feet. I reached the passenger side door and swung it open in excitement and nervousness only to be surprised that the only person there was Brian. He motioned

for me to get in. I jumped in to get out of the cold and out of sight in the night. I was thinking, "Maybe the others were delayed and we were going to get them?" He said, "The others cancelled, so it's just me and you tonight." I was disappointed and nervous. I didn't know Brian that well but then thought that Brian and I could have fun anyway.

He drove around to the back of the neighboring empty house, and we walked in. There was no electricity, so I looked for the room that had the most moonlight. It was a bedroom on the front of the house. Brian had brought a Ghetto blaster, and we spent the first few minutes getting settled. We talked somewhat awkwardly for a little while. He knew I was an athletic trainer for the football team and asked if I would give him a massage. He took his shirt off and laid on the floor. I wasn't really excited about this, but it gave me something to do with my nervous energy, so I agreed. Next thing I knew he asked for me to do his legs, so he took his pants off and laid back down. I hesitantly continued. He was super skinny, not like the football players I usually worked on. He looked strange laying there in his underwear and smelling like cigarette smoke with a thick layer of cologne. I continued.

After a few minutes, he said, "It's your turn now," and convinced me to let him massage me. First, just my back, then, all of a sudden, he undid my bra strap saying, "Oh, it was in the way." Then he convinced me to let him massage my legs. I was still nervous but naively didn't think much about it. Massaging others was a normal part of my life. Why shouldn't I let someone massage me? There was no harm in a massage, but then he started kissing my back. "Whoa! What is happening?" I thought. This is not a massage, but maybe he didn't know any better. He asked me to roll over. I laid there in my underwear with a thousand questions in my head too afraid to voice any of them. I didn't like this. I didn't like Brian like this. What was happening? Next, he took off my underwear and climbed on top of me. He asked if I wanted him. I said, "No." He asked if I wanted to have sex. I said, "No." I didn't want to be there. Why didn't he stop when I said no? I laid there silently paralyzed in the moment studying the feeling of my first sexual intercourse with a man. I was surprised at how much it really didn't feel good. I had thought about intercourse and always imagined that it would be pleasurable.

He would ask me, "Do you like it?" I said, "No." "Do you want me to stop?" I said, "Yes." I don't know how long we laid there, the floor hard against my back, the carpet course, the smell of cigarette smoke covered by cologne and the 'Dirty Dancing' soundtrack playing in the background. I just laid there with him getting sweaty against my skin, and his cigarette smoke smell all over me. "Do you like it?" he said. I said, "No." He said, "Do you want me to stop?" I said, "Yes." Then finally, he did. He rolled over on the carpet near me, exhausted in his efforts. After a few minutes, he laid next to me, wrapping himself around me, telling me how much he liked me.

I dressed feeling betrayed by the evening and angry at Amy for leaving me alone. We got dressed. Brian kissed me goodbye. I walked through neighbors' yards in the dark and snuck back into my bedroom anxiously awaiting a hot shower in the morning to get this dirty smell off of me. The questions loomed in my mind; What just happened? Why didn't I fight? Did I love him? I just gave him my virginity. I must love him....but deep inside I also hated myself....because I just laid there.....because I let it happen....because I snuck out in the first place....because I didn't fight.

Rocking forward, she dropped the paper on the deck and said, "Well, there it is. It's out there. I got it over with." Then she began to really rock back and forth while looking off into the blue sky. Everyone sat there in a moment of silence and waited to let her steam dissipate.

Greg was afraid this was how the story would go. For Lisa, a cloud of shame came over her with the night her cousin, also named Brian, was like this.

Brock wanted to throw up and felt like his chest was caving in. This was almost identical to one of his drunken, college escapades after a frat party with a "girl next door." He has carried haunting guilt and shame for thirty-five years over it and has been tormented with thoughts of what happened to the girl. As tears ran down his face, he spoke first. "Angela, I am so sorry this happened to you. This was so wrong what he did to you. You didn't deserve that."

Angela said, "Thanks, but I should've known better. What kind of clueless girl wouldn't have seen what was going on? The next day at school I saw Brian coming down the hall, and he darted into the bathroom. I know he saw me. I didn't see him the rest of the day, and the next day when I ran into him, he just said, 'Hey, how you doing?' and kept walking. Sure, he liked me alright. I was such a fool."

Francie spoke, "Angela, this is clearly a serious event, but why did you choose this story?"

With a sarcastic grin and gleam in her eye she said, "After this, I felt so dirty, I just decided who gives a damn. I'm already a tramp, so I just decided to keep going. One guy to the next until I was twenty. Then Paul got me pregnant, and I dropped out of college."

Greg and Lisa asked a few questions about her parents, Amy, and the cologne, but no one was really sure where this was going. It seemed to be going nowhere as every question led to an answer of Angela condemning herself. Finally, no one wanted to ask questions for fear of it making things worse.

After a long time of silence, to ease the tension in his mind, Greg imagined himself yelling as loud as he could.

Francie finally asked, "So, Angela, was this your first sexual experience?"

Angela's eyes bugged out, and she stared at Francie and thinking, "Who the hell are you to ask me that question?" It was the one question she didn't want anyone to ask. "No," she said. Then she exhaled really big, leaned back, and seemed to in a moment, change from a bitter woman to a soft, young girl. Then she spoke. "When I was ten, my cousins lived in the same neighborhood. Stacy was my age, and I really looked up to her. She may have been eleven, but no matter what, she knew a lot more about life and things than I did. One day, she wanted to play a new kissing game with me in the attic room of her house. My mom and dad would kiss me, and she was my cousin, so I didn't think much of it." She paused as she began to get nervous.

Francie said, "How brave to share this with us."

Angela decided to go on. "Stacy told me she would teach me about boys and girls and the birds and the bees. She said we had to take our clothes off. She went first, so I did next. She told me what to do and had me kiss her all over. All over." Tears began to fall as she put her head down and continued, "This is the story I wanted to write, but I just couldn't do it."

"Angela, we are about out of time, but I need you to look at me. This is a really great place for you and very important. We are going to come back to this tomorrow, but this story with Stacy is directly related to the one you wrote about Brian. Stacy made you feel special and then took advantage of you. This was sexual abuse even though you were girls and only children. You brought the story of Brian to us and have spent most of the time blaming yourself. There is no way anyone here could blame this ten-year-old little girl."

Everyone at the same time said, "No." Then, they waited for a good while for a red Cardinal to finish singing on the fence line. Everyone watched and took it in like a dance coming to an end. Angela sat far back in her rocker with tears dripping from her cheeks onto her coat.

"Well done, Angela. I am so proud of you. This is good, really good. Now breathe."

She did and looked at Francie with a smile. When the group saw Angela's smile, everyone knew that victory was just beyond sight and not just for Angela but for everyone. Francie rocked back and spoke, "All right, you all are amazing; now take a deep breath." Everyone did. "I know our work is not finished, but I am proud of each one of you. I look forward to being back together tomorrow. Now, it's about 4:30, and you have free time until dinner at 6:30. You can take a nap, go for a hike, play a game, or whatever you like. However, there is one critical thing; as hard is it may be for some of you, there can be no discussing your particular story with anyone outside of group time. What happens in group, stays in group."

After a moment of thinking about what Francie just said, everyone felt a sense of relief that free time would not included anyone trying to fix anyone. They all stood up, and Greg headed to the bathroom. Brock began lighting a cigarette while walking to the fire pit once more. Lisa walked the other direction toward the pasture, and Angela sat back down in her rocking chair and wrapped herself with Lisa's blanket and began to rock.

Football to Morning Glories

Before long, Greg, John, and Rob converged on the fire pit and threw a few large logs on to keep it going for later that night. Greg asked, "So what are you guys going to do for free time?"

As John gazed at the fire, "Well, I sure wish I knew the score to the SEC Championship game right now. Man, I've never made a decision to give up tickets to a game for something like this." He paused. "But, I've gone to eleven seasons of games, and honestly I may only remember a few of them."

Rob said, "Well, did anyone bring a football?"

Greg perked up, "There is a bin on the back deck with Frisbees, balls, and other stuff. Let me go see what I can find."

Within a few minutes, the three of them were throwing a youth size football and pretending to catch winning touchdowns. John kept quiet about his shoulder hurting. Rob was not able to throw it nearly as far as Greg and John. But then, in the imaginary end-zone, Greg ran and dove to catch a Hail-Mary pass. At that moment, all three of them were pumped up and felt like real pros. Then they took a break.

Angela and Karen had connected within minutes of arriving on Friday night. They both had lived in the same town in different years but had gone to the same elementary school with the same teachers. Coming to the retreat from different states, within the first hour, they bonded like second grade classmates.

Karen was hanging out in the living room, waiting for Angela's group to finish in hopes of going for a walk. When Karen saw they had finished, she went out to the deck and found Angela curled up in her rocking chair. "Hey girl, how are you? Can I sit down?"
"Sure," Angela responded.

"I was kind of hanging out waiting to see if you might want to go for a walk with me."

"That sounds great. Give me a minute to put on my walking shoes and a sweatshirt."

They got up and headed out, but before they had even reached the main road, they had already stopped several times to look at a groundhog in the field and chipmunks on a woodpile. The biggest excitement for Karen was showing Angela every wildflower they came across. Karen knew all about flowers from her grandma. Angela had never noticed flowers much, but today, as Karen handed them to her one-by-one to make a little bouquet, it was if her eyes had been opened, and she was seeing flowers for the first time. As the bouquet grew, so did her amazement of how no two flowers were alike. Even ones of the same kind were so different. Halfway down the cedar-lined road was a horse pasture. When Karen and Angela walked down to the fence line, three of the horses immediately came to them. A brown mare even galloped. Karen, then Angela, scrambled to pull up grass from their side of the fence. When they were done feeding the horses, they stood back gazing at the beautiful creatures, and for a moment both of them wished the retreat would never end.

By now, Ryan and Brock had decided to burn another cigarette together and to check out the old sawmill. Ryan was freezing because he didn't bring any cold weather clothes, but Brock had an extra farm work coat in his truck. Brock gave a warning, "Man, I'm sorry, but this coat smells like tobacco. I threw it in the washer at home and didn't realize I had left a brand-new pack of cigarettes in the pocket. It was a frickin' mess. I pretty much had to tear apart my washer to try and clean it all out. I washed that coat three more times, and it still smells like tobacco."

"No problem. It's thick and warm, and that's all that matters to me. Boy, you're right; it does smell like tobacco. Clean tobacco," Ryan chuckled, and they both laughed.

Then Brock added, "Yeah, if we run out of cigarettes, you and I can gather around my coat and light it on fire." Then they really laughed.

When they made it out to the sawmill, both of them were amazed and excited. The sawmill blade was four feet in diameter, completely rusted

but still sharp. There was a large pile of rough lumber next to it for some other project that didn't get finished. Brock scrambled to look around to figure out a way to fire it up. He found an electric motor cord, but it clearly required a power generator from somewhere else. Brock seemed to know a lot about things like sawmills, so Ryan began to ask questions. The questions began with how the lodge was built, then to tractors, then to the NASA space shuttle, and after an hour, they spent the rest of their time talking about women. For both of them, the hour they spent together was priceless.

At the beginning of free time, Francie quickly did some prep for the hamburger and hot dog cookout. Mary and Lisa wanted to help. Francie prepared fresh coleslaw, Lisa sliced tomatoes and washed lettuce, and Mary got the pot of baked beans going and the sliced cheese ready for the grilling. "Many hands make light work," Mary affirmed.

They each expressed their lack of desire to be outside in the cold, so Francie brought up, "How about we play some Scrabble?" Lisa was in, but Mary did not like games much. But, if she were to play a game it would be Scrabble. She was good with words and spelling. After they got well into the game, each of the players' styles and strategies became evident. Lisa had poker experience from game nights at college, so Francie and Mary had no idea what Lisa was going to do next. Francie and Mary both were very methodical players. After much intense thought, each play was like a great revealing of something magnificent. Even when it wasn't. Francie loved to play games. Any games. Growing up in Northern Illinois, there were many fun nights and girl talk with her grandma she loved so much. Mary mostly didn't like games because she hated losing in front of people. But this time seemed different. For the first time since Mary could remember, she didn't care about winning or losing; she was just enjoying playing.

Dinner

The sun began to set over the mountain ridge, so Greg and John got the grill fired up. This was John's world now. It was as if he was having his friends over for tailgating after a championship football game. Everyone began to trickle back into the lodge. Greg got the inside fire going, and Ryan had fresh hot coffee brewing. There were only three hamburgers that got burned up, but five Ball Park dogs were so black Greg launched them into the darkness of the night. Greg hadn't been paying attention on Friday night when Francie made the announcement about not leaving food outside.

Everyone was super hungry, and most talked about how great the burgers were cooked to perfection. Several shared how fun it was to have hot dogs that they hadn't had in a long time. Everyone turned to watch Brock pick up his masterpiece hot dog, covered with baked beans and heavy mustard and began to take his first bite. John said, "Wow!" as the mustard and beans poured off the dog down Brock's white goatee. Brock stood up from his seat laughing, and everyone else joined in.

Laughing, Brock said, "This is how we do it in Texas. Go big or go home."

They laughed some more as Brock went to wash up. As they all turned back to eat their food, everyone, even the women, were thinking how glad they were not to have a big, white goatee.

Nearing the end of dinner, Francie spoke up, "Alright, here's the deal for tonight. In a few minutes we are going to clean up, get coffee, play a fun game for a little while, and then we will all bundle up and head out to the fire."

Ryan asked, "So, I brought a few cigars from home. Are we allowed to have a cigar by the fire tonight?"

"Sure," Francie smiled, "as long as you brought one for me." Rob's group laughed, but the rest, after being in group with her, actually could imagine her firing up a cigar. It was a mystery, but no one knew for sure.

Every person sprung into action, helping to clean up. Brock, Greg, and John did dishes, Lisa and Mary stored the leftovers, Angela wiped the table and counters, Karen checked the outside fire, and Ryan made a backup pot of coffee. Francie and Rob got the table ready for game time and some music going.

Over the next hour they played Catch Phrase. A few people had played it before, but most had not. Francie had people sit in specific seats. Every other person around the table was from her Story Group, and the opposite people were from Rob's. In the middle of the table sat a very annoying timer that was loud. The timer sometimes lasted long and sometimes not so long. Then there was a little word machine that produced random words in a little glass window. The goal was to give clues to your teammates for them to guess the word you got. Then, when someone on your team guessed it, you would pass it like a hot potato to the person next to you, and the machine would give them a new word. Whoever got stuck with the word machine when the timer went off lost, and the other team got a point. The first team to twelve would win.

Francie was excited, but Rob was thinking, "We would never do this at a men's retreat. Oh well, it will be interesting playing a game fueled by pressure and anxiety after such an intense day."

So, they began. The first few turns were quiet. But, by the time it got to Angela, halfway around the table, people were laughing so hard they could barely hear. After a couple rounds, the score was tied at eleven, and it was Karen's turn for the win. She hit the button, and the word "circus" popped up. Karen was so serious about the game that she jumped up from the table and started sounding and acting like a chimpanzee! Then, she did elephant noises! Next, she was roaring like a lion! Her team guessed everything they could imagine, except "circus." As the final buzz sounded, she sat down exhausted. Both teams clapped for her like they had been watching an actual circus act. "Bravo, bravo!" John cheered.

Football to Morning Glories

Francie grabbed the game box, "All right, it's time for S'mores."

"Oh wow," Mary said, "I haven't had S'mores in years and years. How fun!"

Ryan went to his room and dug in his duffle bag. A couple minutes later he brought out a package of chocolate chip cookies to share with everyone. Francie noticed, "So, Ryan, cookies? Nice. Where's my cigar?"

Ryan paused and stared at her serious face. "Well, I'll go get 'em. Give me a second." He left. Ryan rifled through his duffle bag again to find his cigar box. He had brought just five. He wasn't planning on any women smoking a cigar. That had never crossed his mind. He returned to the kitchen with his box, cut the end of a cigar at the table, and said, "Here you go."

Francie stressed, "Now, I only smoke good ones. Is this a good one?"

Ryan began to panic a bit. "I was in Miami last year, and a guy on the beach sold me these and said they were high quality from Miami."

Francie spoke with sophisticated eloquence, "I usually only smoke Cuban cigars from Havana. I've not heard of a Miami cigar. Hmmm..."

Ryan didn't know what to say as he stood there.

After a long pondering look, she finally confessed, "Ryan, I've never smoked a real cigar. I'm just playing with you."

He was relieved, "You! You really had me going. I was gettin' nervous. Honestly, I didn't bring enough for women, too. It didn't even cross my mind, and I was freaking out. When I was digging under my bed, I thought, 'Maybe all the women want cigars? I don't know. Maybe women smoke cigars at these retreats?' Oh Francie, you're killin' me."

All the women were laughing as they headed outside.

By the time the women and Ryan arrived at the fire, John had gotten long sticks for roasting marshmallows, and Greg was already handing out graham crackers and chocolate.

"Where are my graham crackers?" Greg inquired.

"It fell on the ground over there," John responded with a smirk.

When Karen came out to the fire, she was prepared. Built into the bill of her new camouflage cap were LED lights that came on with one squeeze of the bill. Problem solved. Quickly everyone got what they needed, and the roasting began. Rob and Greg liked to catch their marshmallows on fire. "Burned black is perfect!" Greg said.

Mary chimed in, "Slow and steady. Nice and brown. That's the way a S'more should be done."

"I'll take chocolate anyway I can get it. Just toss me one of those bars. I can make a S'more after I have some chocolate," Angela said.

Ryan spoke up, "Toss me one, too."

After everyone had their first round, they began to settle into their seats around the fire. Several made another S'more, but most had had their fill. Brock reached down deep in his coat and pulled out a thick, plastic bag. "Well, I brought some homemade beef jerky from Texas. My neighbor raises cattle, and once a year we get together and make smoked jerky from ribeye." He passed it around, and everyone took a piece.

"Wow, this is really good," John said.

Brock explained, "The key to beef jerky is fresh beef and fresh spices. We grow the peppers and dry them for the mix."

Greg spoke up, "Mary, we need to start making beef jerky like this at home."

93

Football to Morning Glories

She smirked and raised her head, "You mean I need to start making beef jerky for you."

Others chuckled and laughed except Greg and Mary. Uncomfortable, Greg got up to grab another log to hide his embarrassment, and Mary, with her hands in her coat pockets, continued staring at the fire, stone cold.

When Greg stood up, so did Rob. "I'll be right back," Rob mentioned as he walked toward the lodge.

He headed inside the lodge, went to the men's bunk room, got down on the floor, and pulled out a paper bag from under his bed. Before heading back out, he grabbed a lighter from on top of the mantle. Walking through the dark toward the light, he stopped halfway and called for Francie to meet him. "Francie, I need you for a second." Nervously, she came over, and he said, "Ok. I have a surprise for you, and no one else needs to know about it if you would rather not do this. It's perfectly ok." He held up the paper sack. "On the way here I picked up some simple fun fireworks. A few packages of morning glory sparklers for all of us to do together. After I heard last week you were going to do your barn story, I thought, just maybe, you would be open to it?"

Francie's heart skipped a beat with fear and excitement at the same time. Rob stood there and waited patiently for her to think about it.

"People will think sparklers are silly," Francie said with hesitation.

Reassuringly, Rob commented, "No, these kinds are pretty fun, and everyone will love it."

"Ok, I'm ok with it, but you'll have to lead it. I'm not," declared Francie.

Then, Francie went back to her seat. Because Mary also had a story with fireworks, he needed to talk to her as well. Rob asked her to meet him. He explained the same thing to her. She had done Morning Glories with her own kids, and it was fun. "Well, nobody's drunk. Let's do it," she said as she rolled her eyes with a smile.

They both walked over to the fire, sat down, and Rob put the sack under his chair and waited for a pause in conversations that were going on.

A while later, Rob said, "Well, I brought a surprise for everyone. I asked Francie and Mary about it, and they're all in. I brought some fun fireworks, just Morning Glories. I thought anyone who wants to can."

Every face lit up around the fire. It was exciting, and everyone knew this was a really big deal. Followed by seven other responses just like it, John said, "I'm in."

"All right then, let's go out here in the open field," Angela directed. "I love Morning Glories with all the beautiful colors, and they don't burn you like regular sparklers."

Greg helped open the packages and pass them out. Everyone gathered around Brock who held the lighter. Francie went first. Then Mary. Everyone else then scrambled to get theirs lit. Within thirty seconds, there were ten Morning Glories lighting up the night sky. Lisa and Karen began to run in the field. John waved his in a circle standing still. Greg held his straight up high, pretending to be the Statue of Liberty. Everyone else set out to write their names, words, and shapes in the night sky. It was a sight to behold.

The red-hot embers from the fire and lights from the lodge were out by midnight.

Be Present

Today was a sleep in day. Breakfast was at 8:30, an extra thirty minutes. John and Angela were, as usual, up with the chickens, but everyone else stayed sound asleep all night. When Francie's alarm went off, Karen pulled her blanket over her head and went back to sleep. Five minutes before the breakfast blessing, Angela went and woke Karen up again.

Karen hadn't slept so well and so much since she could remember. She rolled out of bed, slid on her clothes, including her hat, brushed her teeth, and headed to join the group waiting for her. When she came through the door, all eyes were on Karen. "Good morning!" she said. Most eyes opened wide being captivated by Karen's appearance. Something had changed. Her eyes and face even glowed, looking years younger.

Lisa said the blessing and everyone dug in.

Breakfast was quickly ending, and the second pot of coffee was strong. Rob and Lisa had snuck without Ryan knowing and made it just the way they liked it. Ryan noticed and teased, "Hey, what's going on? Have I been fired? It's a terrible paying job, and the work environment is horrible. I was going to quit anyway."

Everyone laughed as Ryan got the volunteer job jokes going. Greg was next as the fire man. He stood with his hands on his hips and serious, "Let me tell ya, when I applied for the campfire job, it took three interviews. They talked it all up. Before you know it, I'm working for the man. No safety equipment. No wood-hauling cart. No chainsaw or splitter. Just an ax. And then I've got to keep up with two fires. One inside and one out. Nobody told me that. I'm gonna form a union."

As everyone laughed, Mary was smiling, proud of her witty husband. Brock and Angela had tears from laughing so hard. It made it more hilarious that

Greg never broke character, not even a smile as John muttered, "This is serious, I hope he doesn't go on strike."

As Brock tried to contain his laughter, he put his hand on his stomach, "I can't do it anymore. My abs are killing me. I'm going to pull a muscle."

Bringing everyone back to order, Francie instructed, "All right. Let's get cleaned up. You know the drill. Five minutes to be in your seats."

Everyone scrambled and got settled in as Greg quickly threw another log in the fireplace.

Rob kicked it off, "Good morning everyone. We want to start off this morning with a few important requests as we begin the day. First, you have all done well, very well so far, and we did some heavy lifting yesterday, but today is just as significant as yesterday. We are not done." Then he turned and looked at Francie.

"I want to make something very clear to everyone." Everyone looked up as Francie looked at each person's face, one-by-one. "We need you here today. Now, and all day. One of the main reasons we have made the progress we have is because each of you have been fully present. Don't leave us now. Don't pack yet. As soon as someone begins to pack or talks about being back home or checks their phone, you and others are already leaving. Gone. Rob and I are asking you to stay here with us. Mind, body, and spirit until 3pm."

Half of the group felt energized. The others sat back in their seats with the realization that they had already left. They were already thinking about the loneliness or pressures of returning home. Lisa couldn't believe Francie's insight. As of five minutes ago, Lisa had been in front of the bathroom sink, looking in the mirror, sick to her stomach with anxiety from imagining returning to her cold, empty house. Greg's mind drifted back and forth, wondering if the drive home with Mary would be fun or a fight.

Transitioning, Rob explained what was happening next. Well, now we're going to break up for some quiet time alone. We are giving you some story reflection questions to consider. During your private time, read your story again, reflect on what happened in group yesterday, and answer the questions. Do your best as this will be your map for group time later."

Lunch was grab-and-go deli sandwiches, chips, and vegetables. People could take their lunch to spend more time outside working on their assignment.

With the sun shining so bright, everyone was excited to go outside. Angela took a blanket out into the open field and spread it out to lay on.

Greg went hiking up into the woods, looking for a log or something to sit on. About twenty yards up the wooded, east mountainside, he ran straight into an old tree swing. The ropes and wooden seat had molded, but it was still strong. Greg felt like he had found a hidden treasure and decided to swing for a while before doing his work. He felt alive.

John carried a rocking chair over his shoulders far out into the field, facing the cow pasture, and Karen went and laid down to journal in her bed. All of them found their own special place.

After an hour, Francie rang the bell outside the door to give the five-minute warning. As everyone trickled in, Rob announced, "Alright, everyone, use the bathroom if you need to, then go ahead to your group. My group is going to meet outside today at the opposite end of the deck."

John agreed, "That sounds great!"

The morning reflection time was of great value for everyone in one way or another. In the bathroom looking in the mirror this time, Lisa was present, focused, and on a mission. Brock was excited to get back with his brigade, but Mary was anxious, teetering between hope and fear. Everyone else was in between.

South Corner

John and Ryan gathered rocking chairs to bring to the south corner nook of the lodge deck. Mary, Rob, and Karen arrived and all sat down.

"A rocking chair. I love rocking chairs," Karen said as she rocked back and forth.

"What a beautiful day," John declared.

The group sat there pensive, feeling the time slipping away as they hung on to the challenge of staying present.

"Well, here we are back together again. Let's start off with doing a check in on where you are as we head into our time together. John, let's start with you."

"I'm having a great day so far. Breakfast and private time like that is something I never do. I'm at the plant at 5am every day including Saturdays. Being with you all and being forced to take time for me was life-changing. I didn't even check my phone to see who won the game yesterday. Nobody tell me if you know. I'm recording it," he said with a smile.

Karen went next, "I don't know what it is about this place, but I don't think I've ever slept that well my whole life. And nobody gave me a hard time or got stressed out for me sleeping in. I don't know. I don't know what any of this means for me, but I am hopeful that my life's going to change. I'm not sure how, but it won't be the same. It has already. I feel different."

Almost under his breath, Ryan said, "Karen, you even look different," and everyone agreed.

"I do?" They all nodded. "Well, I'll be darned," she responded with a surprised look on her face.

Ryan began, "I had a great time with Brock yesterday. We hung out at the sawmill and talked about a lot of things and laughed a lot. He's a funny guy. I know I'm young and everything, but the fact is, I don't hang out with men much. Growing up with my mom and grandma, being around men has not been normal for me. Part of me coming to the co-ed retreat was the comfort of knowing there would be women here, too. Men have always given me a little more anxiety. I have learned so much. And, I just love this group. This whole experience. I'm still shocked about what Mary said yesterday about me being a dad someday. That was good to hear. I thought about that in my bed last night before I fell asleep. I'm looking forward to this today."

Everyone smiled and thanked Ryan. They all felt a deep, sacred honor of witnessing this young man growing up this weekend.

"Ok, I'm not feeling that great," Mary admitted. "I feel like there's a lot of pressure to figure all this out before I go home. There was some really good stuff from yesterday, but I need answers. A direction. I know I need to be patient, but it's just hard. I've got to tell ya, I even told someone while chit-chatting Friday night that I had a pretty good childhood. Ha! I really believed that. I suppose I had to believe that just to survive. Oh, well. Now what? This has been eye opening, and I know it's not all going to get fixed by 3 o'clock, but you said it's about progress. Well, I'm making progress alright. I just don't know what direction."

"Thank you, Mary. Speaking of progress," Rob said with a smile, "it's time for us to get started, and we'll go in the same order as yesterday, so we will start with you Mary."

Mary – Take 2

"Ok, here goes. The first question I addressed was about themes in my story. These are themes I came up with: danger, alone, afraid, and unnoticed."

Rob probed, "Anyone have anything to add for Mary?"

"Well, curiosity, smart, desire, attention to detail," John proposed.

Ryan said, "A sense of right and wrong. Listener."

With a hint of a smile, Karen added, "Adventurer. You seemed to naturally go from place to place looking around for adventure. You even perked up on doing the robot talk into the fan with your cousin. I got the sense from you and your story that you saw everything as a possible adventure to be had. Everyone else's adventure was destructive."

Mary wrote down all these other themes she hadn't seen at all but admitted, "I just thought we were supposed to write down the negative things." Everyone knew she was so critical of herself, she had a hard time seeing or believing the positive ones. But she scrambled to write them down and even read them off to make sure she didn't miss anything. She thought, "I'll have to study all that later."

"What's next?" Rob asked.

"Well, what did I lose in this story? I lost being a twelve-year-old girl. Everywhere I turned was a dangerous or nasty adult world. Often, my dad was drinking. My mom was always watching him just to cover up him being drunk. She would pick up after him and make excuses when he would offend somebody. No one was looking out for me."

Looking around the group, Rob invited, "Anyone else?"

"It must have been tough not knowing much about sex. You were probably caught in a lot of situations that were embarrassing," Karen mentioned sympathetically.

Mary raised her voice, "You can say that again! Especially at school!"

There was other sharing and reflecting on the family drinking, sexuality, lack of close friends, and not fitting in.

Then it was quiet while Rob pondered a moment, "Well, Mary, I know we talked about Bonnie's room yesterday and sex and so on, and that is important. But after thinking more about it, it seems there is something else lingering in this story." Mary gazed at Rob, waiting. "The dialog. You never said a word or were asked anything about yourself. I feel like the biggest thing that was stolen from you was your voice. No one was even interested in you. And I mean you."

Mary sat frozen as tears welled up.

As the tears began to run, she got passionate, "Yeah, I don't know why no one seemed to notice me. They were all too busy, I guess. That's why it's so damn uncomfortable for me to sit here right now. This whole weekend people have actually asked me questions, and on top of that, listened to me answer. It's been unnerving. Like in this group. You all are looking at me and listening to me. It's all I can do to get through it."

John was shocked to hear Mary say "damn," and Ryan thought it was awesome and grinned.

Karen said, "Girl, you have more to offer than what you think. What you said yesterday to Ryan about having kids, I was thinking it but never would have said it. You did!"

Being vulnerable himself, Ryan admitted, "And I gotta say, when you said that to me yesterday, it changed me. Like ripping a log-jam out of my life."

She knew what they were saying was true but couldn't make sense of it.

John said, "Mary." She looked over to him. "Your words have power," he said and then paused. She froze again. "I've noticed all weekend that you've been quiet, and that's not really a surprise to understand now, but it's also been clear to me that when you do speak, it has significance. It's not like me when I get to rambling about things that really don't matter. Yeah, it's true. Your words have power."

Everyone chimed in their agreement.

Mary sunk down in her seat and stopped breathing for a few seconds. "Well, that's interesting. I will have to think about that one." She sat there in a daze of shock, thinking, "These are the most honest people I've ever met. This must be true. Oh, my."

Rob stepped in, "Mary, as we come to a close, you said at the beginning you wanted direction and answers. Where are you now?"

Mary pondered and then spoke, "Frankly, I was not expecting this. Finding my voice. That is so scary, but at least now I know the real reason I am stuck in my life. And stuck in most every part of it because not having a voice affects everything."

Rob acknowledged, "Often when a person doesn't believe they have a voice, it's because they've come to believe they are of less value than others."

Mary stopped breathing as though she'd been caught.

Rob continued, "So they keep quiet, and it slowly builds up bitterness. It can get bad enough that a person begins to not even like themselves."

Mary thought, "Oh my, that's me."

Rob finished, "Mary, you were given a voice that must be brought into this world, and as John said, it is a powerful one."

Mary's face put off a glow as she sat there. Then they all sat back in their rocking chairs as though they had crossed a finish line.

Rob exclaimed, "Alright, let's hear it for Mary!" and they all clapped. Mary smiled.

After a brief silence, Rob spoke, "Who's next?"

"That's me," John said.

"Great. Let's do it."

John – Take 2

"So, here we go. Themes in my story are fear, anger, being trapped, and perfectionism," John shared.

"Anyone else?" Rob inquired.

Ryan quickly spoke up, "Yeah, confidence. At ten, you were the first to stand up to say the pledge. That's pretty cool."

"Writer. Your story was very well-written. Survivor, perseverance, overcomer. Look at what you are doing now. This would have ruined a lot of people's lives. It's amazing," Mary said with assurance.

With a gentle smile Karen voiced, "Courage. You said you're afraid to speak in front of people. You've had no problem here with us. You seemed like a guy who had it all together, and at first I even wondered why you were here. Your courage and fighting for your life has taught me a lot. A lot about myself. Thanks, John Glass." As Karen finished with a smile, John grinned back and put his head down.

The group discussed parenting, speaking in public, his brother, then John said, "As I thought about this story and my time at Oak Park, I began to realize that it did end up forcing me to have really good study habits and be more responsible. I pay attention to details that most people don't notice. The problem has been the fear that follows me like a dark cloud. As I thought about it, the more successful our company has become, the worse I've gotten. Like if I make a mistake, it will be catastrophic. Getting awards has even made me sick to my stomach. We're just making steel not doing brain surgery," he said as he shook his head.

Ryan suggested, "So in some ways, it's kinda like you are still at school."

John got quiet, sat back, and turned his head toward the field. "I suppose I am still at school."

With John having the gaze of a traveler stuck at a train station, Karen said, "Maybe it's time to leave."

In a bit of a fog, John replied, "Yeah, maybe it is."

Rob spoke up, "John, you have really gotten to an exciting but scary place today. Your challenge has become what does it mean to leave the school? Do you graduate? Do you just walk out? In many ways, that ten-year-old is still there waiting for someone to come and pick him up." John sat back listening. "There is only one person who would understand. Only one person who would know just what to say. No one else can go back and get him. I can't. We can't. Your parents can't. You're the only one. You have to. The good news is that you are in charge now, and you know best what he needs. I know for sure, just sitting next to him a while would be a great start."

John sat there in his chair, a thousand miles away imagining standing in his old classroom doorway. He could see the boy sitting at his desk. Waiting. He glanced in his mind's eye at the the empty desk next to him.

Then everyone said, "Thanks, John."

Mary took a drink of her sweet tea, and Ryan picked up his bottled water. "Well, Karen. I think you're up next," Rob said.

Karen – Take 2

"Well, I've got to say first thing, that I'm not sure I did this right."

With her book on her lap, everyone could see her book was almost solid blue ink from writing so much. John sat up, ready for Karen's report, and Mary put her tea back down under her chair.

"First, I only wrote a few themes, but I also wrote out what they meant to me. I loved talking about my Mimi, but you said to go back and review your actual story. The one thing that stood out was my desire to be wanted. So, unwanted was a theme. Everyone's lives were so messed up that there really wasn't room for me and Tammy. I just wanted someone to want me. I can see how that also got me into so much trouble with men later on. I just did anything I could to get someone to want me. I was an 'A' student, a hard worker, a good listener. Here I'm ten, my mom dies, and I immediately start cooking, cleaning, and taking care of grown adults. Still no one wanted me."

Ryan didn't seem to catch that in her story. He was focused on the crisis of her mom's death, and John figured the silver bullet solution to it all was Mimi. Mary was daydreaming of the comfort of the cows in Karen's story.

Karen continued, "Homeless. I really didn't have a home like other people. I just got shuffled around. When we moved in with mom in Strawberry Plains, that was my dream come true. I finally had a home. The truth is, Todd and I have lived in the same house for twenty-five years, and something will happen with his job, and I immediately get afraid of losing our home or having to move. Todd's had several big job offers out of town over the years, but I just couldn't move. The thought of it gave me severe anxiety. Now I know why."

Karen went on to other subjects, and they explored more about her dad, the funeral, and how she had to change schools again a week after her mom died.

Then Rob softly motioned, "Karen, I am so sorry to interrupt. You are doing great, but I'd like to go way back to the 'unwanted' theme for a second."

Mary chimed in, "Yeah. Good."

Rob began, "You are definitely right about being wanted and valued, but I think there is a twist that is important for you to explore. It makes sense for any of us to feel wanted, but there is also something else that is a deep longing we carry. And that is the desire 'to be seen.' For someone to really 'see' you, to know you." Karen raised her eyebrows and put her head down. "But the catch is this; at the same time, one of our worst fears is also to be seen, so we try and hide. So in your story, in one single day, you went from being seen as the smart, new girl at school to the girl whose mom died. In one single Valentine's day, proud to be seen but too ashamed to be seen. You just wanted someone to see 'you,' just you."

Karen began tapping her toes on the deck.
  Quietly, Rob said, "Karen."

"What?" she said with her head still down.

"Will you look up at me?" Rob asked. She paused, then slowly looked up at him. "We see you now. I see you. And you are amazing. Absolutely, amazing." With wide, open eyes, she stared at him. Rob could sense the others shaking their heads in agreement. "Now Karen, I know you can do this, but I'd like you to look at everyone in our group."

She said, "Ughh. You're killing me." They all gazed at Karen with amazement as she slowly looked at Ryan, then Mary, and finally John. Then she sat far back in her chair and rocked.

Everyone sat back and was quiet for a moment while Karen rocked. Finally, after reflecting some, she spoke, "Well, thanks everyone. This is hard stuff. I do, and I don't want to be seen all at the same time. That's a tough spot, but it's where I live. And then, I have all kinds of ways I hide. I act tough, keep my nose in books, stay busy at church, and work until I can barely move. If I sit still long enough, maybe someone will have a chance to notice me. Imagine that."

Everyone could almost see rays of hope, bright above Karen.

She added, "I've got to say, last night around the fire, I thought a lot about my Mimi. I was in complete shock as to how my life and even I am so much like her. I have my own garden and even greenhouse, grandkids live with us, and I even love power tools! Isn't that wild." Everyone chuckled.

They all said, "Thanks, Karen."

Ryan – Take 2

"Well, here we are, Ryan. Three survivors, and you are up next," John said.

"Ryan, you ready?" Rob chimed in.

Ryan responded, "Let's do it."

Again, Ryan leaned forward in his seat and pulled out his folded-up booklet from his back pocket and put his elbows on his knees.

Just as Ryan began to speak, John was distracted with something over the crest of the grassy hill. As John stared, Ryan kept reading. Karen noticed John and looked herself. Rob was tempted to look up but didn't want to be rude as he assumed it was a car. Mary didn't notice as she was the only one completely tuned in to Ryan's sharing.

Then John interrupted, "Hey, hey, I'm really sorry but there are bears coming this way."

Walking out of the woods toward the lodge was a mama bear and her cub. Mary turned. Rob didn't know what to do but sit still and wait. The bears kept coming.

With a bit of caution and wonder, Rob whispered, "In five years of retreats here, we've never seen a bear, let alone bears coming to the lodge. We can watch but be prepared to go inside if we need to. I need to tell the other group." Rob slowly and quietly walked the length of the deck to the other group. When Brock looked up to see Rob coming toward them, he saw the bears in the distance. "Oh, wow. Bears."

The group stood up to look around the corner before Rob even got there. Rob whispered, "Hey, you guys, check this out but be prepared to go inside."

Francie said in a hushed tone, "We've never had this happen. Oh, wow."

Greg began to get a sick feeling in his stomach.

Just then, about forty yards from the deck, the mama bear stopped and began to eat something. Greg muttered, "Oh no. It's the hot dogs." Francie looked at him then back at the bears. "I burned up a few last night and threw them in the field. That's where I threw them." Sure enough, the bear was eating the black hot dogs while the cub stayed close.

In silence, everyone watched the majestic sight of these two creatures. When she was done eating, the mama bear looked up toward everyone, nudged her cub toward the woods, and off they went as quietly as they came. Everyone stayed so quiet they could hear the bears feet breaking sticks and rustling leaves up the side of the mountain. And then, they were gone.

Everyone returned to their seats with a breath of fresh air like after a school field trip. "That was something special, for sure," Karen said.

John smiled, "Yes, you don't see that every day. Well Ryan, frankly, I did not hear anything you shared. I think we should start from the beginning."

Everyone agreed, and Ryan said, "Sounds good to me. All right, let's try it again. Starting off with themes to my story: Dad, dreams, playing, shame, being a winner. Then, what was lost? For that..."

Rob interrupted, "Hold on. Anyone else on the themes in Ryan's story?"

John spoke up, "There was one thing that struck me from your story, and that was the word 'normal.' I think it ended with 'pretending that everything was normal.' I'm not sure what to make of that?"

Ryan explained, "Well, the truth is that's who I am. Always pretending that everything is fine. It drives Christine nuts. I've always just wanted to be normal. I've spent so much of my life pretending, and I don't even know why. Hiding, I suppose."

Rob questioned, "So let's spend a few minutes on what John has brought up. This is pretty important. So, what is 'normal' to you and how would you describe someone who is?"
Ryan got a puzzled look on his face, sat back, crossed his arms, and rubbed his chin. "Well, I don't know. When I got here Friday night, you all seemed normal. Honestly, I felt like I didn't fit in and even thought about leaving. And now after getting to know everyone here, I don't want to leave. It's obvious that everyone has their own story, and the more I think about it, I suppose there's no such thing as normal."

Still searching for clarity, Ryan sat there puzzled about all this. Then Rob weighed in. "Ok. You're getting somewhere, but let's now step into this shame theme. So as you think about your story, where specifically did shame come?"

Ryan recounted the story in his mind. "When my car stopped on the track in front of everyone."

Rob affirmed, "Yep. Now let's think about this. What would have happened if only you, your brother, mom, and grandma were there?"

"Well, I suppose we would have just picked it up and talked about how to make it better."

"Like you would do with Legos and other things. Right?" Rob questioned.

"Yeah."

"So it was the fact that all these people were watching that made you quit because you did decide to quit after that."

"I guess."

Rob went on, "A couple other things to think about. How many cars raced that day?"

Ryan answered, "Over fifty."

Again, Rob asked, "So how many trophies were there?"

"Just five," Ryan answered.

"So then, the vast majority of boys there were also losers?"

"Yeah, I suppose so. I hadn't really thought about it like that," Ryan responded.

"Ryan, here's the even bigger thing about this place you're at in this story. The car stopping was where shame came in, but when it came up that you didn't have a dad, that's when you wanted to get out of there."

Silence came, and then Ryan spoke. "It's true. It was like, all of a sudden, everyone knew my dad left us. I just wanted to run away." A tear began to come.

Rob continued, "So this is where we are with this. You said yesterday, 'Nothing was ever the same after this.' Well, the result in this story is that you quit something you loved. I don't know, but I would guess that maybe you've quit or ran away from a lot of things like this. Good things that you really love."

Ryan sat silent with his head down staring at the floor. Finally, he looked up and began to speak. "I never said it to anyone, not my mom, grandma, or even my brother Brian, but the truth is from that day on I never wanted to be in a situation where you needed a dad to fit in. So I chose other things. Like the whole, 'soccer mom' thing. It's not so obvious to not have a dad with soccer or track. But I decided I would never play football or basketball or be in the band. Every time our school would have senior night at an event, kids would go out on the field or court with their mom and dad. I swore I would never be one of those guys out there with no dad in front of the whole world."

No one made a sound while Ryan took his last drink of water and crushed his empty bottle. In the silence of the group, the crushing of the bottle sounded more like a car crash.

After a few silent moments and Ryan with his arms crossed sitting far back in his rocker, Rob spoke. "It's an honor that you have shared this with us, and sorry seems like such an empty word, but honestly, Ryan, that's all I can say. I am so sorry."

With a blank stare to the field and rocking, Ryan responded, "It's ok."

Looking straight into Ryan's eyes, Rob said, "Ryan, this is really important. With all this and going back to the Pinewood Derby, what got stolen were your dreams of being in the winner's circle. But here is the catch. In order to be in the winner's circle, you have to enter the race."

He responded, "I suppose you're right."

John spoke up, "And it's not big deal decisions. It's everyday decisions. But look at this. Even at your age, you made a decision to come here this weekend, and this is big, really big, and look at you now as you are rolling into the winner's circle right here, right now." Every face lit up and voiced or nodded in agreement waiting for Ryan's response.

Ryan sat back with eyes sparkling and slowly smiled, "Yeah. Yeah. It feels pretty good. Really good."

They all took a deep breath and sat back.

Ryan looked at everyone and said, "Thanks, guys. Thanks, ladies." After Ryan looked at each person with his charming smile, they all sat far back, rocked, and gazed at the sun-filled grassy field.

A warm breeze came, and Karen said in awe, "I can't believe it. I've never seen bears like that."

North Corner

During the fall, the sun shines bright on the north side of the lodge. Lisa loved every inch of sun. Angela moved her chair to shade her eyes, and Brock put his jacket on the deck to sport his t-shirt. Greg couldn't imagine how Francie was wearing two sweaters in the warm sun, but he was ready to get started.

Francie dug in, "Alright everyone. Let's do a check-in. Who wants to start us off?"

Lisa began, "I am as present as I can be. This morning when you let us have it on staying present, I was already long gone. I couldn't believe what you were saying. It was like I had been caught. It seemed so obvious you were talking to me. During my quiet time, it seriously made me think about how much I do that in the rest of my life. I think I do it a lot; leave before something good is even over. In fact, at parties or girls' nights out, I am the first one to leave and tell everyone, 'I have to get going.' And I have nowhere to go! I just feel like I need to leave. But I'm here now. Right here. Let's do this."

Lisa's words stirred everyone to think about themselves as they paused a moment.

Then Francie spoke up, "Well, I don't want to interrupt here, but Lisa has stirred something really important that I want each of you to consider. In fact, you may want to write this down to reflect on later."

Everyone scrambled to grab their booklet and pens.

She continued, "Write this down about endings." She spoke slowly as they wrote, "Everyone has a way in which they end. Everything in life."

They all looked up with eyes raised. Brock said, "Hmmm."

Angela, "Well I'll be darned."

Francie went on, "Based on the story of your life, from the time you were young, each of us have developed ways in which we end. A phone call, a letter, lunch with a friend, a date, this weekend...Will you be the first to leave. Last? Will you turn on your cell phone and radio as soon as you get into your car? Or will you put the windows down and drive slower than usual and breathe? You all know exactly what I am talking about. I will give you a moment to consider. How will you end this time we have spent this weekend? How do you want it to end?"

Greg gazed off at the cows thinking of the many times he has had bad endings. He reflected, "Even the way I get off the phone with Mary is rude half the time."

Lisa admitted she's addicted to checking the time and wondered what it would be like not to wear her watch.

Being on the farm by himself, Brock never wants anything to end when he is around other people. He already knew he would be the last to leave the lodge, but no matter what, the weekend will end with him alone again.

It set in on Angela that most departures from home include an argument with at least one of her daughters. "That can't continue," she thought and then said, "Thanks, Francie. That's good. Really good."

Everyone agreed.

"Ok, who's next," Francie prompted.

Greg stepped up, "I'll go. I've been stressing about the ride home with Mary actually. I don't know how it's going to be. We did what you guys asked and haven't really talked about anything this weekend. We've just had our own space which has been really good but hard at the same time. I've seen her in a different light. That's for sure. Yesterday's group time was great, but I have no idea what's going to happen next."

As Greg's last word ended, Angela began, "I feel stuck. Like I opened a can of worms. I mean, you said yesterday, Francie, you were excited and hopeful, but I don't know. I'm open, but it seems like any light at the end of a tunnel is very far off right now." Then, she just sat there.

"Thanks, Angela," Francie said.

As he leaned back in his rocking chair, Brock spoke up, "Well, y'all, this has been great for me. I had no idea how things would go at a co-ed retreat. In fact on the drive here, as I thought about it, I knew a sexual story was the one kind of story I was not going to get into. Isn't that crazy. I already feel like a thousand pounds are off my shoulders... I still can't believe how you all cared for me yesterday. I just knew I was going to be rejected, and I wasn't. Boy was I wrong. Thank you all."

Everyone felt content about the weekend as they smiled and turned to Francie as she spoke, "Well, I will tell you all. It's getting to a place of 'feeling pretty good,' that valuable ground is lost or stolen. I come to this place as a warrior ready for battle. We did well yesterday, but there is still more ground to be taken back." They all seemed to wake up in surprise, and as young soldiers do, they sat straight up and put on their armor.

Francie continued, "Here we are. We will go in the same order as yesterday, so it will be Brock, Lisa, Greg, and Angela."

She continued, "Angela, Greg, I know it's hard to wait, but we need you to try to be present with Brock and Lisa now, just like we're going to need them when it's your turn. It's taken all of us to get here, and it will take all of us to finish. Alright. We ready?"

Brock – Take 2

As he picked up his papers, Brock said, "Let's do it. Well, the first thing here was the themes in my story. This is what I came up with. Adventure...gone

wrong that is," he said with a smile. "Excitement, curiosity, and shame."
Then he looked up.

Francie spoke up, "Ok, that's a great start. You covered the ones I was
thinking. Did anyone else notice others in Brock's story? Brock, you're
welcome to jot these down."

"Motorcycles," Greg said. "I'm not sure that's a theme, but I love
motorcycles. Friends for sure. Sounds like you had several friends back
then."

Angela chimed in, "Belonging. There was a sense I had the whole time that
there was a deep desire to belong. To fit in. It's been the same this
weekend."

"Yep, true. That's a good one," Brock responded.

For this occasion and before the chance passed, Lisa stretched out of her
comfort zone, "Guys is a theme. There weren't any girls or women in your
story. Except the porn." Then she looked down.

"Hmmm, that's an interesting one. Thanks," Brock responded as he wrote
quickly, convinced that was surely important.

"Anyone else?" Francie inquired. "Nope. Alright, Brock, what's next?"

"What were lies I came to believe? This was a good one. Here's what I got.
One. That this is what it means to be a real man. Two. This is what normal
people do. Three. This is what girls and women want from a guy. Finally,
that this is when people really love each other."

Francie commented, "So from those dead-on answers, what you will now
need to explore is the truth to those lies. So... What is a real man? What
do women want from a man? What does it mean to love someone? These
are some of the most critical questions a twelve-year-old boy must have
answers to. It's usually answered by his dad, but if not, a boy will find
answers one way or the other."

North Corner

Brock, with a surprised look, said, "Those are three questions that I have never actually asked myself or anyone else. I can't believe I was married for twenty-five years and never asked Joanne what she wanted from a man. What an idiot."

Brock caught himself just before Francie stopped, "Ok. So you have made progress, and an idiot you are not. I haven't met a warrior who is an idiot. In fact, that's a great transition to something very critical."

The whole group leaned in to focus.

Continuing on, Francie said, "Most people's lives are spent focusing on trying to figure out what is 'wrong with me,' and it was your words yesterday of, 'You are a f****ing freak' that really stuck with me. I know it was your ex-wife's words, but yesterday they were your words. In working with people, I've found that is all upside down." Francie had everyone's attention. "Let's climb back up into the hayloft for a few minutes. Is that ok?" she asked.

"Sure," Brock said as they all returned in their minds to being back there, sitting on the floor with piles of magazines everywhere.

Francie sat straight up as if to pull her sword from its sheath, "I'd like to focus a bit on the things that are right with you, Brock. Boys are born to be curious, so that's perfectly normal. That curiosity mostly moves our world forward but sometimes causes trouble. There was a question on where did the anger or sadness come in, but I want to ask you now, where did shame come into your story? And I really want you to think about this. Skim back through your story if you need to."

Brock turned back the pages to his handwritten story. With his goatee like a pencil to the paper, he scanned and scanned. After scanning the whole thing, "I don't know. I can't figure it out."

Like a laser beam, Francie declared, "Because there was none in the story." He was shocked, and the rest of the group perplexed. "You are going to need to follow me on this. It's really important. In your story, you said, going down the ladder, you felt like what?" she asked.

"Like I was alive," he answered.

She went on, "Yep, and that's exactly how a twelve-year-old boy should have felt. When a young boy or man sees a beautiful woman, his body is supposed to come alive or rather, we say be aroused. It's the way you were made. The problem comes in when the way you were made gets twisted or marred by evil. Also, a boy and man are stimulated with their eyes by what they see. Women are aroused by emotions and connection. If a girl had been there, she would have had a desire to talk with you instead of look at those magazines."

Brock said as though pieces of a puzzle were coming together, "I see where you are going. That makes sense."

"Well, it is time to transition, but I do want to finish with this. There is more to be explored in this story that will require spending more time in the hayloft. We have talked about the magazines and porn which is important, but frankly, you learned as much and were impacted even more by Mark because he was real. Male or female, another person being sexually aroused in front of you is an extremely powerful thing. To make it more significant, you looked up to him. Many of your sexuality questions of manhood were actually answered by Mark and not those magazines."
Brock sat there with his mind swirling and stunned along with the rest of the group. After hearing Francie say this out loud, he knew this was true. Like a fast flashing slideshow, he reflected on his many trips to the hayloft and being around Mark the following years.

He said, "Yeah. You're right. I'm going to have to spend some more time on this."

Francie concluded, "This is good. Really good. Every good story deserves about two months of exploration. It's not a quick weekend and then move on with your life. It's like peeling back an onion. But, it is not a never-ending onion. There is always something new you can discover, but I have a couple stories that I could barely even read at first. In fact, one of my hardest stories I began to explore with groups two years ago, and now that story has so much less power over me that it doesn't make sense to share in groups. I suppose you could say there comes a point of diminishing returns with exploring a story."

After what they had experienced so far, that made perfect sense and gave them each a great hope. Even Angela.

They all said, "Thanks, Brock."

As he chuckled, he said, "Boy, I could use a cigarette now!" Everyone laughed.

Angela didn't laugh so much. She was getting hot, and her stomach tightening up. Her head wouldn't stop spinning thinking about herself and her cousin, Stacy. "What does all this mean?" kept swirling in her mind.

Francie knew from Brock's story, that Angela would be far away from the group at this point. "Greg, Brock, are we ready?"

Looking right at Angela who was in a fog, Francie asked, "Angela, are you with me?"

Angela came back and sat up. "Yes, I'm right here," she said.

"Good," Francie said. "Lisa, you're next."

Lisa – Take 2

Francie kicked it off first, "Before you get started, Lisa, I wanted to follow up with something from yesterday. It's actually a clinical thing I thought I would share about being 'frozen.'"

Lisa looked up with attention and a pen in hand, "Ok. Let's have it."

"In your story, you referred to being 'frozen,' and you really seemed to be troubled by it. 'I just stood there frozen,' you said."

"Yes, go on," Lisa prompted with curiosity.

"Well, during times of trauma, and frankly, leaving your friends and your best friend, Catherine, was traumatic. To protect ourselves when bad things are happening, we have a chemical or hormone called cortisol. Most refer to it as our fight or flight hormone, but there is another state rarely taught. It's really fight, flight, or freeze. In survival mode, the surge of cortisol and other hormones makes us feel pumped up to fight. Well, that doesn't fit with Catherine in the hall. Flight or running away didn't make sense either, so being stuck in between fighting and running away is literally freezing. Like leaving your body. An out-of-body experience."

Lisa lit up, "That's exactly what it was like. An out-of-body experience."

Francie smiled and responded, "And that's what happened right here in our group yesterday. You were afraid to share this story and sharing the pain of the loss of Catherine made it seem like it was happening all over again. So when you were done sharing you said, 'See, I'm doing it again. I don't even know why I'm crying.' You know, we have a daughter and son, and sometimes Rob and I will begin to get into an argument, and you know what they will do?"

"What?" Lisa responded.

"More often than not, they will start singing or humming or making some kind of random noises. They literally go off into another world right there at the dinner table. It's a common way children and us adults protect ourselves. We were made that way. People can call it checking out if they want, but it's a bit more neurologically complex than that." Francie said as she laughed, "I get a kick out of all that brain stuff. It's really not my forte, but I know a few of the big words here and there."

Lisa shared, "That is helpful. I check out a lot. Now I get it. I can pay attention to that. I've thought there's just something wrong with me, but I guess instead, the fact is, there is something right with me. What about that!"

Francie smiled and nodded, "Well, now that is out of the way. Lisa, let's dig in on your reflection work."

"So what were themes in my story? Change, friends, crying, shock, I'm not sure if you can call that a theme, but that was a big part of it. And family. That's what I've got," Lisa shared.

"Very good. Ok. Anyone else?" Francie asked.

Angela piped up first, "Positive. You seemed to have a positive outlook on life. Even when it was tough." She paused, and then said, "Determined. Then and now even bringing this story that has bothered you, you've been determined to figure this out. To not give up, actually on Catherine or yourself, I suppose."

Brock didn't think of other themes but shared a couple things about growing up with his sisters and then asked about boy relationships in her life. Lisa seemed to blow off his boy question by making fun of her fourth grade kiss with a boy named Carl, being stuck going to a prom with her cousin, and her lack of success on ChristianMingle.com. It was awkward for everyone else to watch Lisa make fun of herself and rattling off a resume of failures.

Francie just listened and waited. They all sat there quiet, and it felt like no one knew what to do.

The silence was killing Greg. He only had one thought on his mind, and he was determined not to say anything. Then he broke. After a deep breath, he said, "Alright. I'm not sure how to say this, and I hope I don't offend you. But I wanted to say the word 'luggage,' but that sounds kinda bad. I guess to say it in other words, I just got the sense that you lived like you were just drug along behind everyone else. Even here, there's been a feel and even comments from you that you are less important than the rest of us. And frankly, it's just not true, Lisa."

With such a raw statement from Greg, Lisa hung on every word with her soft eyes as big as saucers. She couldn't believe Greg was saying these things. For a moment with tears flowing, she couldn't breathe. Silence returned, and she turned to look out into the cow pasture where several black cows were eating at the fence line.

"Luggage," she finally muttered. "That's a perfect word for how I've felt my whole life. And you said it. You said it for me. It's out there. I've been living inside pull-behind, luggage. Yep. And now I'm trying to grow up, and I don't know how not to. I sit around waiting for someone to come and drag me along. It's all I've known. With four older siblings, I was always the last to be noticed, 'to be seen' Francie calls it. Ha!" She looked off and quiet came again along with a black bull mooing, and then a red heifer joined in.

Brock sat quiet, twiddling his goatee and then offering up some insight, "I might be off on this, but one of our questions was something like if there has been any good in your life come from the bad in your story. You just nailed it. I've been trying to name what it is that is so unique about you. And that's it. You see people. You notice people. You know what it's like not to be noticed. That's how you make people feel so special."

Lisa sat far back in her rocker, and a half grin cracked.

Brock lit up, "Isn't it funny how it's pretty much a catch 22. The more we've gone through your story, the more we've come to actually 'see you.' You, Lisa. Yeah, you."

Everyone smiled in amazement while Lisa blushed with everyone looking at her. She rocked back and forth with half discomfort and half excitement.

Angela added, "Yeah, we see you, girl. Right here, right now. Beautiful, I love it!"

Lisa rocked back and said, "Ha, you guys are killing me. No more hiding from this group. You've all caught me."

Francie moved to close. "This is really good and you have been caught. But your challenge becomes in dealing with what we call ambivalence. Again, where you are stuck. You hate not being noticed and yet are frightened to be noticed, to be seen all at the same time."

Francie waved one hand toward herself and one hand away and said, "Yes, like I want you to come close but not too close. I want you to see me, but not too much. It's become easy for you to hide. But Lisa, this group has now torn the locks off the luggage with you, and they are broken. Your luggage is useless now. You are going to have to come out to be seen. So you are going to need some more exploring the ways you hide and push in to those areas that are uncomfortable."

Francie took a risk, "Like, for instance, has there really been no guys interested in you online?"

With her eyes bugging out, Lisa responded, "Not exactly 'none.'"

Francie pressed on, "So how many? Do you have a number?"

She mumbled with her head down, "A couple dozen probably."

Everyone sat back. Brock breathed heavy with a feeling of relief. Greg thought, "Of course. Now that makes sense." And Angela smiled, saying in her mind, "Oh yeah, now that's my girl!"

Lisa exclaimed, "Ok. Ok. I get it. It's time now. It's time. I get it, but it's scary. I've got no luggage. It's also pretty exciting." With a smile, she sat up straight. Everyone smiled, and then Lisa laughed, "I hate luggage."

Everyone else laughed and said, "Thanks, Lisa."

Greg – Take 2

Greg had thought a lot about his turn. Even while he was in the woods swinging during reflection time, the whole subject about being stupid was really bothering him.

Greg began with rising blood pressure and volume, "Ok, my themes. Stupid, champion, stupid, adventure, stupid. There are several themes in my story, but I've been so troubled since yesterday over this stupid thing. My dad called me stupid all the time. I guess I just came to believe it. In fact, I'm really sorry I got angry in group, Lisa. Here you were just trying to help me. I was so determined to prove to you all that I'm stupid that I even started yelling." He stopped there and put his elbows on his knees and his face in his hands.

There was a tension in the air with everyone not knowing how Greg was going to walk through this. They looked at Greg, then Francie. After letting Greg sit there a moment, Francie began, "Greg," then she waited for him until he sat up. "I must say, we can all see the passion of a champion fighting to win. Right here, right now."

In a single moment, that truth turned tension into excitement for the whole group. They became members of a pit crew at a big race. Brock went from being nervous to it feeling cool to sit with a real champion. Lisa accepted his apology in silence and was ready to get back to work, and Angela admired this unbridled passion and wished she could be more like him.

Greg didn't know what to say. He was ashamed for losing it. Francie was amazed with his passionate fight. Greg didn't know who was right, he or Francie. "I'm not sure how you can say that," he said.

Francie answered, "Frankly, I just see the real you. The you I've seen the whole weekend serving others. Bringing your wife to this retreat was a real risk for your marriage, and you knew it before you came. You have not missed a beat in caring for the fire, and I heard you guys at the grill talking about your diving, Hail-Mary football catch. These are all marks of a champion."

Brock spoke in a low voice, "Greg, I'm sorry bro. But it's pretty obvious that you're a champion."

"Maybe a bit rough around the edges, but a champion for sure," Lisa confessed.

Angela said, leaning back with Greg now looking right at her, "It's funny. It was obvious when you were done 'going off,' you were ashamed with your head down, and here I'm sitting thinking, 'Wow, I wish I was more like this guy.' All at the same time. Ha! That's crazy."

Greg's head was spinning, being the only one blind to himself.

Francie took the lead with her passion growing with every sentence, "Greg, here's the deal. We all see this in you. You're smart, caring, competitive, determined, compassionate, and that's just a start. But what we all think about you doesn't matter. I could sit here all day long and talk about the great things about you, and I've only known you for twenty-four waking hours. We could take turns in this circle for twenty minutes listing off the great things we see, but it will do no good. None at all. It's a complete waste of time as long as you continue to hate yourself." Silence dropped like a hammer. There was one creak in the board under Brock's chair.

Angela thought Greg might get angry about Francie's statement. Hate seemed like a huge word to Lisa, but Greg, sitting straight up was stone cold, frozen. Everyone was on edge. Waiting. Greg began to tremble a bit as he said, "No, I really don't like myself." It was like a balloon burst. Then he muttered again, "I don't."

Francie responded with a grin of hope, "Hmmm, now we're getting somewhere. This is good, Greg. This is really good. Thank you for being honest with all of us."

Angela couldn't wait to see what would happen next. Lisa was thinking that the answer must be Greg needing counseling, and Brock was hit hard with the same feelings of hatred about himself. "And this is somehow good?" Brock thought.

Greg went on, "Ok. I can see and hear the nice things you are saying, and if it was someone else you were talking about, I would agree with the rest of you. But the way I feel about myself is so deeply ingrained. Like all the things you said, I have a negative version in my head. Like, I yelled at someone in my group. I couldn't even start a fire Friday night. I'm too out of shape to play sports, and my marriage will probably get worse after this. You see what I mean."

Francie paused to decide what to do next. "Ok, Greg. Here goes. I'm going to let you in on some things, and it's some of that brain science stuff. And you're going to have to stick with me on this and not jump to the left or right."

Greg pleaded, "Alright. I'm in bad shape. Whatever it is, bring it."

"Ok. You shared with us that your dad called you stupid often. Correct?"

"Yep," he chirped.

"Well, at a young age, your brain is developing, and I mean growing, literally growing at a rate that is 4 to 8 times that of an adult. That's why kids can learn other languages when they are young, and it's so difficult when you get older. Anyway. When someone, especially in a position of authority says something like, 'You're stupid,' it tends to have a more significant impact than when you are, say, eighteen. Does that make sense?"

"Sure. Yeah, it does," he replied.

Angela began to scramble thinking about the things she says to her daughters.

"In fact, if it was a hundred times or just one significant time, it can be very critical in what you come to believe about yourself. So, let's say it was just once in second grade, then the next day you struggle in writing class. Now, why are you struggling and other kids aren't?" she asked him.

Looking perplexed and with hesitation he said, "Because I'm stupid?"

"That would be a logical conclusion for an eight-year-old after being told that. You see? But was it true?"

Thinking about not doing so good in second grade, Greg mumbled, "Uhhh. I'm not sure."

Francie went on, "Greg, we all, including you, concluded yesterday that you are in fact, a smart person, so it cannot be that you were stupid. Now let me get to the point of all this."

Greg said, "Ok," as he tried to wake up a bit.

"Your dad may have only said this a few times or many. I don't know, but your dad is not the point or helpful to dwell on. So, blame your dad, then what? Ok, fine. Dad, it's your fault. Now what? Listen, there is one person that has caused you more harm than anyone else in the world. Who is that Greg?" she asked as she lifted her brow.

Staring right at Francie, "Me," he admitted.

"That is correct."

That profound statement landed solid on everyone in the group.

"For every one time your dad or someone called you stupid, I would guess that you have called yourself that a hundred times. And every time you do that, it is like lifting weights and working out to build muscle, but you are actually strengthening brain circuits that have recorded, 'I am stupid.'

"Wow, that makes sense," Greg started to perk up.

"So this is what happened yesterday. We put you in what's called a bind. That's where there are two competing thoughts, literal brain circuits in your head, and you don't know which one to choose. Yesterday in group, you called yourself stupid, and you also admitted to being smart. You even looked like you were getting dizzy in your seat while you were struggling to answer. We waited a long time, but we were not going to give up until you named the truth. Now, you said, 'Maybe...I am smart,' and I let the 'maybe' go. It was progress. That dizzy feeling was likely the negative brain cell circuits letting go. Literally dying."

"I was dizzy. After group, I was completely exhausted," he said as began to see light at the end of his tunnel.

Francie went on, "Neurologically, it is important to speak truth out loud. Just thinking is not that helpful. When you speak out loud it actually grows more brain cells. If you are going to recover from this, you will need to be naming truth to combat these lies you've told yourself, and you also will need others to help you, starting with Mary." He was feeling pretty good about himself thinking they were done, then she said, "Here's a tough one for you, Greg."

He grinned with his head up, "What's that?"

Like a professor, she propped her chin on her hand and inquired, "Are you a champion, Greg?"

He shrugged his shoulders and said, "Sure."

"No, Greg. I asked, are you a champion?" she said again with a bit more intensity.

He sat up straight a bit confused.

"Yeah. Yes," he muttered.

"Yes, what, Greg? Yes, what?" she asked.

"I am a champion," he said quietly.

"I couldn't hear you," she admonished.

He began to think she was crazy. "I am a champion!"

"I don't think everyone could hear you, Greg," she said once more .

Finally, Greg caught on, let loose his passion, and with the same mannerism as Evel Knievel, put his arms in the air and cried out, "I AM A CHAMPION!"

Then he doubled over and laughed hard while everyone clapped. Brock howled, "Woohoo!" and Lisa did a finger whistle. Angela laughed until she cried from joy and from the angst of being next.

Francie smiled, and when they finished, she said, "Thanks, Greg."

Angela – Take 2

Francie looked at Angela and smiled. This time, she already had her papers in hand. Angela started to stand up as if to leave and said, "Well, I have learned so much from all of your stories, I think that will give me enough to go on. I'm in good shape. Is that ok Francie?" Then she sat back down and laughed. Everyone else just smiled, knowing there was still a heavy battle ahead.

Francie smiled, but with clear focus said to Angela, "Well, I wish it could be that easy, but we still have progress to make, and we wouldn't want to leave that girl back in her room alone. It just wouldn't be right, would it?"

Angela scrambled to look at her papers and replied, "Nope. It sure wouldn't."

Brock felt his stomach pounding, hoping for a miracle to heal Angela and the guilt over his own college days. Lisa was looking forward to this as she was confident good things would come. Greg glanced at Angela a couple times, confident she wouldn't mind leaving the girl behind, but Greg thought, "No, not today. Not today!"

Angela started off, "Well, I wasn't sure what to do. I did focus on the story I wrote, but the way things went yesterday, it seemed like I should also look at my story with Stacy? I just wasn't sure, so I did the one I wrote."

Francie just listened then said, "Angela, this is your time. Just share with us what you've got, and then we'll see where we might go. Ok?"

"Alright. Sounds good. So I focused on my 'Guy Next Door' story. Here are the themes I came up with. Deceived, naive, taken advantage of, shame, dirty, lost." Then she looked up, waiting.

The rest of the group kept silent waiting for Francie. "Angela, I want to be kind when I say this, but we need to be very clear here." Angela had a look of innocence on her face. Francie said softly, "You were not taken advantage of. You were sexually harmed by Brian. You were raped by him."

Everyone sat in silence waiting for Angela's response. "Yeah. Yeah, I was."

Francie continued, "Ok. Group, let's name some other themes, and then I have somewhere I'd like for us to go. Ok?" Angela shook her head in agreement.

Brock was ready, "Trust is a theme. You trusted your friends and even Brian. You said naive, but I saw you as a trusting, free-spirited girl, full of life who never thought a best friend's friend was going to abuse or harm her."
Lisa was confident, "Smells. It might sound crazy, but in your story, smells were pretty important. His cologne, cigarette smoke. It really made it seem like we were there."

Francie offered, "Adventure. You were a girl of adventure. You didn't sit idly and wait for life to pass you by. You didn't want to miss anything. You were a girl of adventure."

North Corner

Greg thought for a moment, "Related to the trust thing Brock brought up is caring. At first I thought it was odd, and then I realized it's because I must not care about people as much as you do. But anyway, you were a physical therapist for the school athletes. You're a nurse now, and even in your Stacy story, it didn't bother you when she wanted to play a game where you cared for her body. I'm sorry if that sounded bad," he said with a scared look.

"No, that's really good, Greg. That doesn't bother me. That's great insight. Thanks," she said as she sat back relaxed a bit.

Seeing how that went over well, Francie decided to transition. "Angela, I can see how you are in a tough spot in between the two stories, and we have limited time. In my experience, I think it would be more beneficial if we turned our attention to you and Stacy. Because if we can help Angela at ten, then she will be more equipped for when she is fifteen."

That was the strangest thing most of the group had ever heard. Even stranger was that it seemed to make sense as Greg scratched his head, and it sent Brock back into deep thought, twiddling his beard.

Francie encouraged her, "Angela, as we start, is there anything else you want to share with us about Stacy. And the more you can be specific, the more we might be able to help you."

She began, "Before they moved to our neighborhood, they lived on a farm. She was a farm girl and so different than me. She seemed to know so much more about a lot of real life. Growing up in the city, things were pretty much the same all the time."

The group asked a few questions about going to the same school, her and Stacy's parents, and about other kids in the neighborhood.

Francie drilled down, "How many times did this happen with Stacy?"

"Well, they only lived there a year. It was a Christmas to a Christmas." She began to scoot around a bit in her seat. "It was probably five or six times.

The first few times it was like a game, but then one time, I told her I didn't want to play that game, but she said I had to. If I didn't play the kissing game, she would tell my mom that I was bad and did bad things like stealing, which wasn't true at all. I've done other things in my life, but I've never stole anything. Anyway, so I gave in and played along. I was glad when she finally moved. I saw her at family reunions in the summers until I moved to college. I avoided her as best as I could."

Francie was pensive, "I want to make clear that as hard as it is, the longer we stay away from the attic and the kissing game, the more we don't help Angela." Everyone with eyes wide open shook their heads to agree.

"Angela, let's walk through this. So yesterday, you made clear that with the kissing game, Stacy made you kiss her 'all over.' Right?"

"Yes," Angela spouted.

"And I think we all know what all over means. Is there anywhere you did not kiss her?"

"No," she replied.

With such courage, Greg felt like Angela was beginning to raise her own sword for battle. He was charged.

Francie asked, "Like we talked about earlier today, as you think about those first few games with Stacy, do you recall being ashamed?"

Angela responded, "I actually thought about that when you asked Brock about the hayloft, and the answer is no, I didn't."

"I didn't think there was, so here are a couple critical things for you to consider that are very important. I know you have had counseling on this subject, but not about Stacy, I'm guessing?" Francie asked.

"No, it's never come up because people say you have to be a few years older or a situation more like Brian to be abuse. No one's ever asked until today," she answered.

Francie went on, "Well, there is something similar to Greg and his dad. So, let's say it was sexual abuse with Stacy. Now what? Or it wasn't. Then what? The fact is, it really doesn't matter. What does matter is how it affected you and is affecting you now. Does that make sense?"

"It sure does. I've wasted a lot of time spinning my wheels. One counselor tried to tell me to forget about Brian and move on, and another friend told me I should check out pressing charges against him. Nuts."

Francie pulled it back, "Ok. Back to Stacy. I need to ask you a question. Can you tell us more about what went on with the game in the attic?"

At this point, Angela wasn't afraid or embarrassed and spoke plainly without hesitation. "Sure, we would take off our clothes, she would lay down and have me kiss her all over. The things I will never forget are the noises and the smells. The smell of her entire body, the moaning, the groaning. And she treated me like I was special."
"Then, did she play the kissing game with you?" she asked.

"I honestly don't remember," Angela answered.

Francie said, "That's ok. So here we go. So, what were our bodies made for? Our bodies were made for work and stuff, but just as much our bodies were made for goodness, play, pleasure, and to connect with others. And pleasure doesn't always mean sex, but it can. Listen to me on this. There are more nerve endings in our mouths and our penis and vagina than anywhere else on the human body. Anywhere. It's the way we are made. Yes, for food, procreation and all that, but for pleasure too. So you two playing this game is no surprise, and it's no surprise that there was no shame at first, but there is a catch..."

When the words penis and vagina were spoken, everyone froze and stopped breathing while acting like it was business as usual. After the shock was over, it was somehow liberating. Greg wondered, "When did those words ever become so bad?" as he scratched his head again.

Francie went on, "With sexual harm, it's insidious and complicated because most often, while someone is being harmed, their body is still aroused." Francie raised her elbows, linked her hands together and pulled tight. "In other words, there is a part of the body that is experiencing pleasure, and part that gets tied together and connected with the harm that is going on." She clasped her fingers together and pulled again. "And that all gets wired together in your brain because during times of arousal, almost every firing chemical is running wide open in your body, and in the case of trauma, your brain records it big time as to say, 'Don't ever get yourself in this situation again! DO NOT FORGET! YOUR LIFE DEPENDS ON IT!' So, what happens later? Well...."

Angela interrupted while staring out at the pasture, "Like, every time you start to get excited with your husband, you start to freak out because your body is certain something bad is going to happen. Or your new boyfriend and your next boyfriend thinks you must not actually like them, and they break up with you for instance. I would guess that's what would happen." She now knew why she felt sexually defective for so long.

Francie paused until she knew Angela was done. "Thank you, Angela. The deep shame of sexual harm is often as much over the pleasure of the body as it is the harm. That's why evil targets sexual harm. When you are young, the damage can last a lifetime. The thing is we've never met anyone who wasn't sexually harmed in some way. It just depends on how hard you look. The reason it's such a huge target is because at the end of the day, from birth to before death, we were made for one thing."

Everyone could almost hear the silent drumroll.

"Connection," she said. "Connection. We were made to connect with others, and if our sexuality is harmed, it's the best way to isolate us from intimacy and connection and get us to live or feel isolated and alone. People who have been harmed like this can be surrounded by hundreds of people and feel all alone. Angela, you are a powerful woman and bring so much into this world. It's clear that the best way to take you out is to make you fear getting close to people. And in this case, men and women."

That last comment caused Angela's hair to stand up on her neck. She had focused for so long on male issues and never considered why she didn't feel comfortable with or trust women. "No wonder," she thought.

More quiet sat with them all. Then Angela finally spoke, "Yeah, this is what we were made for. Right here, right now. We were made for connection like this."

More quiet and another creak from under Brock's chair.

Francie smiled, "Indeed we are, Angela. Indeed, we are."

Then Francie began to rock again, and it felt like everyone was putting away their swords. A warm breeze came. Brock and Greg sat still, taking in this last moment. Angela and Lisa rocked with a new hope like fresh, crisp air filling their heavy lungs.

After leaning back in her chair and rocking like a farm girl on her front porch, Francie finished, "It has been such an honor for me with spend this sacred time with you all this weekend." As she looked at each of their faces, smiling, she said, "I am so proud of each of you. You have done well. Very well. The war is not over, but this battle has been won. Much ground has been taken back. I am so proud of you," she said as a tear rolled down her face. "Thank you for allowing me to be part of your story."

She sat back and rocked again, and then so did everyone else. "Well, it's time to head toward the finish line. The other group has finished as well. You have fifteen minutes to pack up your stuff and then be back in your seats for our closing time. Ok."

Everyone nodded.

Brock and Greg said at the same time, "Let's do it."

Ending Well

Francie's group headed inside. Ryan had his sleeping bag on one shoulder and his rucksack on the other. As Francie came through the front door, he was heading to his car out the back door.

"Francie, hey, you need a cigar for the road?" he said with a laugh.

"Only if it's a good one!" she responded.

Rob was picking up empty cups and random trash and then said, "Someone help me move this couch back where it goes." John stepped to the other end to help.

Greg and Mary were tag teaming cleaning up in the kitchen when Brock spouted off with a laugh, "Hey, Greg. Maybe you should just put all the leftovers outside! I bet those bears are still hungry."

Greg rolled his eyes and responded, "Oh, that's a good one." Then he shared with Mary that it was the hot dogs he threw that the bears came to eat.

She was not impressed. "Maybe that's why Francie announced Friday night not to leave any food outside."

"I must have missed that!" Greg responded as he went back to washing the last biscuit baking pan.

Brock was cramming all his clothes into his suitcase and changing out his hiking boots for his cowboy boots. As he got down on the floor and checked under his bed, he got a shocked look on his face and said, "Wow."

"What is it?" Ryan asked.

Ending Well

Brock gazed out his bedside window, "I can't even remember the last time I was this excited to head back home."

Ryan smiled.

Closing

Everyone was back and ready to go when Rob opened, "Ok, the last thirty minutes is what we call preparing for re-entry." That sounded really good to everyone. They were antsy about how to head back into each of their worlds.

"First, we are going back to where we began on Friday night," Rob said and turned to Francie.

"Yep. All of you think back to Friday night to our values for the weekend. Rob said to all of you that there was no way to really understand our values, and that you would have to experience them. Many of you are puzzled right now, thinking, 'What has happened here this weekend?' Well, experiencing these values is exactly what we have done. So you know what we're going to do now?" Francie asked.

Ryan said, "Read them again."

She nodded, "Yep. And we're going to start over here with the five of you, and take your time as you read them out loud. Don't just breeze through them. Ok? John?"

John sat straight up in his leather seat, cleared his throat and began, "Clarity - we seek clarity when we consider the stories of our life that hold confusion. Truth takes back ground that evil steals with whispered lies."

Angela was next, "Honor - as we engage our story and the stories of others, we do so with honor. We honor all that engage their story by loving them where they are. We never push or require more than anyone desires to walk."

Greg continued, "Kindness - as we explore our story and who we are created to be, we engage others and ourselves with kindness. Kindness is what speaks against what evil intends for harm."

Then Lisa, "Safety - we commit to provide a sacred place of comfort and care. We are free to be honest about ourselves and our own emotions. In a safe place we listen and do not interrupt or judge. A safe environment allows what is hidden and breaking through to come into the light."

Finally, Brock, "Growth - when we engage our stories with honor and kindness, finding clarity in a safe environment, there can be exponential growth and impact. This is everyone's desire for each other."

A silence hung in the air as Rob allowed everyone to silently engage their experience of the values. "Ok. Check this out. Let me walk through how cool this is, and this will help you a lot for after you leave here. In fact, I wish everyone could have these tattooed somewhere. Of course, I'm kidding...but kinda not."

He laughed at himself.

"Anyway, here we go. In other words, in order to grow, you need clarity. It's not possible to grow from a state of confusion. Right?" Everyone nodded. "Check this one out. So, it's also not possible to grow while smothering with shame. You must be in a place, environment, or with people where there is honor, or you cannot grow. It's just plain required. Let's go on. Kindness. Same thing. You can't grow in the presence of anger and contempt. You just can't. Especially, anger at who?"
"Yourself," everyone said at the same time.
Francie smiled at these amazing students.

Rob exclaimed, "Exactly! We are our biggest enemy when it comes to contempt. Self-contempt is like poison. How do you be kind to yourself amidst such hard work? You will each have to spend some time reflecting on, 'What does it mean to be kind to yourself?' Even after this retreat. We call it self-care."

Ending Well

John gazed toward the dwindling fire and thought, "I'm going to take paid leave tomorrow. I don't care. That's what I'm doing. And I'm going for a hike with Susan while the kids are at school. Maybe a picnic. She will be in shock." Then a bit of anxiety was overtaken with excitement about the thought of choosing himself.

Karen decided she was going to see if Angela wanted to have dinner close by afterward instead of rushing home. Ryan decided he would not turn on his phone for the whole four-hour drive home and open the sunroof while it was still warm with the heat of the sunshine.

Mary was paralyzed, "That is the most foreign thing I've heard all weekend." The thought of caring for herself was nerve racking. Then Rob gave her a wink of encouragement from across the room. She shook her head. "Oh, Rob Brown, you're killing me," she mumbled as everyone else was thinking hard about their own plans.

"Alright. This is a big one. This is Francie's favorite," he said as Francie took the lead.

"Ok. Safety. The fact is we have established guidelines and structure for you this weekend, and we have a lot of experience in creating a safe environment. We've also been paying close attention as to how to best care for each one of you to keep you and others safe. So outside of here, I would guess most all of you, if you are like us, spend most of your daily life in an unsafe environment."
Ryan spouted, "True dat."

Francie went on, "Some examples. You have friends, coworkers, people at church or wherever, and even family members who are safe and ones who are not. Right?"

They all scanned in their minds their list of people.

"For sure," "Yep," and "Absolutely," came from different people at the same time.

"Some people in your life are just plain toxic. You should think about who you spend your time with. Friends or family who gossip? People who talk about themselves all the time? We all have them. Do you really need to call your mom and listen to her go on about your brothers tonight? Or ever. It will suck the life out of you."

"No doubt," Karen muttered.

Rob offered, "This was radical, but there was one year we were having marriage ups and downs where we couldn't breathe and cancelled Thanksgiving. For us, that's the biggest family gathering of the year. Where we were, we couldn't handle all the dynamics of the holidays, so we called all our extended family and others and told them three days before that we were not having Thanksgiving. We chose us. That was huge. We didn't even cook. We went out to eat. I didn't even have to eat turkey," he said as everyone smiled and chuckled in amazement.

Francie added, "That was a real turning point in committing to safety in our home, marriage, and lives."

Rob went on, "Here's two more examples. Karen, let's say you go home to Todd all excited wanting to tell him all about your weekend, and he's having a beer, covered with grease while working under his car. Then you start talking a mile a minute with excitement, and he says, 'That's nice, honey.' How will that make you feel?"

"Like shit!" she responded loudly. Everyone laughed.

"Exactly. Greg, let's say you and Mary get in the van and ten minutes down the road you start sharing all about your story with a secret agenda to try and get Mary to share hers with you?" Rob prompted.

Greg's eyes were bugging out as he admitted, "Guess what?... I was already planning that in my mind and was thinking it would be a good idea. Wow, not safe. That could have been a disaster."

Mary shook her head in agreement.

Ending Well

Francie picked up there, "Mary may not feel like sharing anything with you until she feels safe or is just plain ready. In fact, she may not be ready to hear your stuff. It might be a good idea to ask in advance or at least say something like, 'Mary, I do have a desire to share some of what I've learned with you, and it would be great if you could let me know when would be a good time.' It may even be best for a date night or after the kids go to bed, just whatever it looks like to create a safe environment with each other. Give her a chance to listen without any expectation of her sharing unless she wants."

Mary nodded positively, this being a foreign and surprisingly good idea, while others were scrambling to jot things down in their books.

Rob moved on, "Ok, if you have been to any type of retreat or workshop before, you know well the 'mountain-top experience.' In fact, many offerings may end up leaving you worse off then when you started. We have resources online that will help you see how and why you can fall in to a place of apathy, fear, crashing, frustration, isolation, or ultimately in despair."

Angela interrupted, "That's how I got here. I found resources online."

Francie transitioned, "Thanks for bringing that up. You can also see in your summary there are blanks to fill in other potential stories. Each of you have explored just one. We've found that each person has six to eight stories between the ages of five and fifteen that have shaped the trajectory of their lives, and ones that represent 80% of what is holding them back in life, and you never really know for sure what they are going to be."

Brock spoke right up, "You got that right!" His group members chuckled.

Rob went on, "How many of you came here with a story in mind?"

Everyone raised their hands.

"How many of you ended up writing a different story than what you originally thought?" Rob asked.

As everyone looked around, all but John had their hands up.

"Wow," Greg groaned.

Francie said, "Ok. Everyone take a moment to write down any other stories that come to mind."

They all wrote bullets fast. After experiencing the stories of others, many had become very clear.

Rob began to close, "One of the last things we want to share is that we've been to things where they want you to come back over and over. That is not us. However, we've told you that each person has 6-8 stories. We recommend exploring three of those in a group or retreat or through coaching or with another friend who knows story exploration. We've found that after working through three over about eighteen months, especially three different types of stories, it will become part of your life, and you will be off and running and even begin to engage others in story work. A friend at lunch, coworker, whoever. Listen, everyone has a story, and they are dying for someone to listen. We all just live in a place believing no one really cares. And as you've experienced this weekend, that's a lie. It's just not true. There are people who care. You just need to have your eyes and ears open."

Mary entered in, "How do you find people to walk with in this? Like, besides Greg."

Francie said, "They are probably in your life already. You just haven't seen it. They may even be people you have stayed away from, and it's because of your own story that you have avoided them."

Mary's eyes bugged out as she immediately thought of three women she has admired but been intimidated by. "I've been afraid of using my voice," she thought. "Thanks, Francie."

Karen spoke up, "My husband gave me the *Look Inside* book."

Ryan added, "My friend sent it to me in the mail. That's how I ended up here. It sat on my end table for six months and kept staring at me until finally I opened it. And here I am. I can't wait to talk with him tomorrow." He was fired up about me coming.

Rob took over, "Speaking of tomorrow, I'm afraid we have come to the end of our time together." He began to get choked up, "I know I can also speak for Francie when I say what an honor it has been to walk with you all. Your courage and trust is beyond words. Even for me, and you all know I have a lot of them."

They all smiled.

He continued, "Well, it's our tradition to all hold hands and have a departing blessing. So, everybody up."

John was asked to say a blessing for safe travels and continued growth for all.

Departure

There were many hugs by all, and a few exchanged contact info. Brock was the first to leave as his truck was packed for a very long drive. He called out, "Y'all come to Texas! Remember, go big or go home 'cause everything's big in Texas!" Everyone shook their heads as he laughed, walking through the open door.

Greg pulled two rolling suitcases and yanked them through the door together. Mary shook her head as she waved and said, "Goodbye, everyone. Goodbye, Moon Shadow."

Karen and Angela were already on the back deck discussing which direction to head to dinner, and John and Ryan shook hands and hugged Rob and Francie. In the blink of an eye, it was Rob and Francie left for the final clean up touches. Rob scooped out the ashes from the fireplace into a bucket, and Francie swept the floor. When the bucket was full, Rob went out the back door to dump the ash into the outdoor fire pit. Dumping it was always fun for Rob because when he did, fine ash would poof up high into the sunny air like a cloud.

When he turned around to head back into the cabin, he was shocked to see that Lisa was sitting on the deck by herself in a rocking chair. He kept to his business, not wanting to interrupt any private time when she called, "You guys need any help?"

Rob smiled and answered, "Nope. I think we're in great shape," as he headed back into the lodge and closed the door.

"Babe, it's strange, but Lisa is outside by herself in a rocking chair. Do you think she's ok? I had wondered where she went."

Francie smiled really big. "Yeah, it's ok. It's definitely ok. Grab those bags, and we're ready to leave. We'll say goodbye to her."

Rob stepped through the door out back as Francie locked the front. He said nervously, "Lisa, I'm really sorry, but we're going to have to lock up."

"No, you guys go ahead. I have everything packed in my car. I'm just going to sit here a while before I take off. Is that ok?" she asked.

Rob and Francie both said at the same time, "Sure," and both gave Lisa a hug goodbye.

As Lisa sat and rocked, the sun was so warm she stood up, took off her jacket, slipped off her sneakers, and sat back down. Gazing out to the mountainside, she could hear the Brown's van rolling through gravel and fading into the distance.

Rocking gently back and forth, she could now only hear the sounds of several little birds chirping, cow hooves walking down the fence line, and the low hum of the warm breeze blowing across the ridges of the tin roof.

Before getting up, Lisa closed her eyes one last time to take it all in.

AFTERWORD & RESOURCES

As you have turned the last page of this novel, you likely have mixed emotions, hope and a bit of uncertainty of what do I do now? Here are some thoughts.

- Journal highlights from your reading experience
- Give a book to a trusted friend to engage story together
- Write your own narrative
- Attend a men only, women only or coed *Story Retreat*.
- Participate in a *Six Week Story Group*
- Visit our resources below

For those who have chosen to take this personal journey of the Moon Shadow Lodge, we have developed some free, follow-on resources for you to access. Such as:

- Healing Path Assessment.pdf
- Specific On-Line Videos from: Brene Brown, Dan Allender, Caroline Leaf, Sentis Brain Animation, Getting Smarter Every Day, Julian Treasure and Scott Musgrave.
- The *StoryFinder* Assessment Survey
- Companion Study Guide

Go to https://www.ClickToLookInside.com

Under Resources > Digging Deeper or Scan Here:

ABOUT THE AUTHORS
Rob Brown

 Rob's passion is transformation. His leadership in corporations, small businesses, groups and with individuals has brought powerful transformation on many levels. He is passionate about growth in every area of life for himself and others. Rob and his wife co-founded *Look Inside Inc*, an organization focused on personal transformation and growth.

Rob grew up in Indiana and met his wife, Francie, at Purdue University where he received a bachelor of science degree. Even while in college, his journey began of working with almost 100 companies in the US and abroad, leading over 500 workshops in twenty years.

In 2010, he began to lead retreats that brought freedom and healing to men dealing with isolation and addiction. These retreats spread across the country and ultimately birthed the organization, *Look Inside* in 2013.

During a year long, intensive program in Seattle, WA under Dr. Dan Allender, he was faced with his own need to grow. It was this experience that catapulted Rob into formal "story-work". He continues to facilitate men and women individually, and in small groups to engage, with honor and kindness, their God-given stories, finding clarity, growth, and kindness.

With Rob's continued passion for transformation, he leads *Look Inside* and is also a speaker, author, and facilitator at retreats and with organizations. He has had the fortune of raising his 4 children with his wife Francie. Their free time activities include hiking and basketball. Their family is growing and they are new grandparents. He and Francie have been married 25 years and live in East Tennessee.

To contact Rob, visit:
www.ClicktoLookInside.com
e: Rob@ClickToLookInside.com

ABOUT THE AUTHORS
Francie Brown

Francie Brown is passionate about people. It is this passion that has propelled her to lead women's ministries, workshops, retreats and to teach her children at home. It is her deep desire to encourage those that she engages to live to their fullest potential. She is passionate about men and women growing into something greater than what even they can imagine.

Francie grew up in Indiana with a heart to teach. She attended Purdue University and received a bachelor's degree in education. It was there that she met her husband, Rob. He and Francie lived in Indiana, Ohio, Alabama and Tennessee as they raised and homeschooled their children. In 2012, she began to lead women's retreats in Tennessee, Minnesota and Indiana then across the country. It was because these retreats began to grow that Rob and Francie co-founded *Look Inside Inc.* delivering almost two hundred retreats.

An intensive year-long training under Dr. Dan Allender in Seattle, WA was rooted in trauma-focused narrative therapy. There, Francie dove into her own story-work that resulted in accelerating her own healing journey. It was this experience that also accelerated Francie's "story-work" with others. She continues to lead women and men with honor and kindness, through their God-given stories, finding clarity, growth, and purpose.

Francie's love of teaching is still evident in her engagements. She co-leads *Look Inside*, leads retreats, speaks and is an author. Francie continues love her children and is thrilled to welcome their new grandchildren. Rob and Francie have been married 25 years and live in East Tennessee. They enjoy hiking and basketball.

To contact Francie visit:
www.ClicktoLookInside.com
e: Francie@ClickToLookInside.com

Made in the USA
Columbia, SC
05 September 2019